In

Friends, Foes & Fools

Fathers Can Teach Their Kids to Know the Difference

James Merritt

PRESS

In a world of...Friends, Foes & Fools
by James Merritt

Printed in the United States of America
Editor: Steve Halliday
Page Design and Typography: TF Designs, Mt. Juliet, TN

Dewey Decimal Classification: 649
Subject Heading:
CHILD REARING / BIBLE O.T. PROVERBS
Library of Congress Card Catalog Number: 97-1478

ISBN 978-1-60647-599-7

Library of Congress Cataloging-in-Publication Data
Merritt, James
    Friends, foes, and fools: fathers can teach their kids to know the difference / James Merritt.
        p. cm.
    Includes bibliographical references.
    1. Fathers—Religious life. 2. Child rearing—Biblical teaching. 3. Parenting—Religious aspects—Christianity. 4. Bible. O. T. Proverbs—Criticism, interpretation, etc. I. Title

www.xulonpress.com

Paying heed to the best of wisdom, and understanding the worst of threats, James Merritt gives answers that can transform the heart of a dad. In a time of broken relationships, here is a book that builds bridges on strong foundations. The joy of committed fatherhood has an unparalleled reward. James Merritt helps us navigate through the perils to win this grand prize of godly children.

Ravi Zacharias, President,
Ravi Zacharias International Ministries,
Norcross, Georgia

Every husband, dad, or homemaker should read this book. I believe it would save a few marriages and help decrease our percentage of "sons without fathers." (To be honest, prospective wives and mothers should read it too.) I enthusiastically recommend *Friends, Foes, and Fools* to fathers everywhere!

Coach Bobby Bowden,
Florida State University Seminole Football

America is a nation awash with knowledge but dangerously lacking in wisdom. Dr. James Merritt points fathers to the source of true wisdom in God's Word. James Merritt is a master expositor, a faithful pastor, and a committed father who not only points the way for other fathers, but models Christian fatherhood himself. By reading this book, fathers will come to know not only the source but also the substance of true wisdom.

R. Albert Mohler Jr., President
The Southern Baptist Theological Seminary,
Louisville, Kentucky

"Exciting, encouraging, informative, and God-centered" describe what Dr. James Merritt has produced in his outstand-

Buy this book for every father you know! It takes the time-tested truths of Proverbs and applies them to the task of fathering in a way that is both helpful and hopeful.

Rick Warren, Pastor
Saddleback Valley Community Church,
Mission Viejo, California

Never in history has it been more difficult or important for men to be good fathers. Unfortunately, most of our culture—from the entertainment industry to government and education—neglects the one book best able to equip men for that role, the Bible. Dr. Merritt, in a very interesting and practical manner, highlights some of its most helpful teachings, particularly the Book of Proverbs. It is a treasure chest of wisdom that will help any man who wants to succeed at the most important role in his life, fatherhood.

Tim and Beverly LaHaye,
Family Life Seminars and Concerned Women
for America, Washington, D.C.

With the wisdom of a Ph.D., the warning of a pastor, the wit of a communicator, and the warmth of a father, James Merritt has written a contemporary classic on the one subject we must not fail—fatherhood. This is must reading for busy men who understand that it profits a man nothing to gain the whole world and lose his children. I personally use this book for my devotions. Having grown up in six broken homes, this book serves to motivate, model, and mentor me in my life quest, being an effective father. I am eternally grateful. I need such a mentor.

Jay Strack,
Jay Strack Association
Orlando, Florida

ing book. It's a why-you-should and how-you-can be the father you need to be guide to raise the son you and God can rejoice over.

Zig Ziglar,
The Zig Ziglar Corporation, Carrollton, Texas

James Merritt is my friend and counselor. Most of all he is a father. . . . His message about child rearing is as simple and straightforward as the Sermon on the Mount or the Golden Rule. He is exactly the right messenger.

Congressman John Linder,
U.S. House of Representatives

Leadership is my heart and passion. The one thing a leader cannot delegate is his family. Using Proverbs as his source, James Merritt has written an outstanding book that will empower every father to lead his children to godly success. It is both powerful in its content and practical in its application. Dad, if you want to read a book that will change you and your family, read this one.

John C. Maxwell, Founder
INJOY

*I dedicate this book to my four best friends:
my sons, James Jr., Jonathan, and Joshua;
and my precious wife, Teresa,
a godly mother who has helped me to raise
three godly sons of whom I am well pleased.*

CONTENTS

xi

Contents

ACKNOWLEDGMENTS

Writing a book must be something like birthing a baby—there is no pain like it, but the product is worth it, at least to the one who endured the process! I have learned that though a book may only have one author, it has many contributors. I want to thank all who made an invaluable contribution to this book.

I am grateful for the confidence that Bucky Rosenbaum and the team at Broadman and Holman Publishers have placed in me in publishing this book. It took a long way around the mountain, but we finally made it.

My research assistant, Michael Cooley, was absolutely invaluable to this project. Thanks, brother, for your patience and input. Now you know if your phone doesn't ring, I'm sick!

My editor, Steve Halliday, is quite simply the best. He is demanding, tough, and honest—everything a writer needs (and hates) in an editor. His suggestions and encouragement were indispensable to the finished project. Beyond that he has become a friend.

Joanne Wardell has been my administrative assistant for the past eleven years. She is absolutely the best. I never would have attempted this book without knowing she would do the typing! I could never thank her enough.

I want to give a special thanks to my good buddy, Zig Ziglar, who took time out of an extremely busy schedule not only to read the entire manuscript, but to spend one and a half hours on the phone with me one Saturday morning. He gave outstanding suggestions and made me feel I was "at the top."

I never would have found the time to write this book if not for my beloved associate pastor, Chuck Allen, who shouldered the load of day-to-day church business, supported by the greatest staff in America. Thanks to all of the wonderful team at the Fellowship of Joy who serve our Lord alongside me.

I am grateful to two wonderful parents, Glenn and Miriam Merritt, who gave me a loving Christian home, took me to church, and taught me the ways of the Lord. No mom or dad is loved more by a son than they are by me; I even get to be their pastor!

My three wonderful sons, James Jr., Jonathan, and Joshua, are the greatest! I love them more than life itself. With them there is never a dull moment, but I wouldn't have it any other way.

Finally, my very best friend and soul mate is my darling wife, Teresa. I still can't figure out why she married me—but thank God she did. If she ever leaves me, I'm going with her! Solomon was right when he said, "A prudent wife is from the LORD" (Prov. 19:14). She certainly is!

May my Father in heaven be glorified in this effort and use it to make all of us fathers more like Him.

INTRODUCTION:
I AM A DAD!

L ouis Sullivan, former Secretary of Health and Human Services, delivered a speech to the Institute of American Values in January of 1991 and made this startling observation: "Though our society is only beginning to recognize it, the greatest family challenge of our era is fatherlessness—male absence from family life. . . . The adverse consequences of a father's absence cannot be reduced to only a decline in income. It is one thing to substitute for a missing father's paycheck. His attention, his guidance, his discipline, and his love, however, are not easily replaced."[1]

Though Sullivan was referring to fathers who are physically absent, I believe we have a problem with fathers who are emotionally and spiritually absent as well. It doesn't matter whether you attend a tiny country church or pastor a megachurch—we all battle this growing problem.

I am a family man and extremely proud of my family. I am neck deep in sons, having three—the oldest is a teenager, the second just became one, and the youngest is trying to act like one. (My wife and I named them Eeeny, Meeny, and Miney because we are having no Mo!)

I trust my fellow dads will appreciate what I am about to say. Life is changing, and fast. My oldest son is a high school senior, my middle son has entered the "Teenage Twilight Zone," and my youngest son is now talking of "going out" with a freckle-faced ponytail with a cute grin rather than going out to shoot hoops. All this has set

1

off emotional sirens, reminding me once again: *I am a dad!* Therefore, I had better get with it, for the sun is setting on the days of my being the primary influence on the lives of my boys.

As I leave the twilight years of being "Daddy" and permanently enter the "Dad" season, I realize how badly I want my sons to be prepared to enter the battlefield of life, armed to the teeth with all of the spiritual and moral weaponry they need to *win,* not just survive. I do not give much thought to how my children might make a living, but how they are going to make a *life.*

That is the reason I write this book: to give what help I can to enable you, my fellow dads, make an eternal difference in the lives of your children. I write as a humble traveler on the same pilgrimage that most dads take, trying to take two steps forward for every one step back.

If this book helps a dad out there step up and become the spiritual leader in his home, get involved in the nitty-gritty business of building character in his children's lives, and motivates him to be the godly dad his children deserve, then I will be blessed and glorify my eternal Father in heaven.

Dad, I think you will agree that in this world of Hollywood morality, Washington ethics, and Harvard thinking, we need all the help we can get! I hope this book will help us all to keep from stumbling as we walk along the path of fatherhood and point us to God's instructions for getting up when we fall.

PART 1

LOOKING UP TO A CRUMBLING DOWN WORLD

Chapter 1

IS THERE A DAD IN THE HOUSE?

*Within the home, fatherhood in our generation
has completed its two-hundred-year march
from the center to the periphery.*

—David Blankenhorn,
Fatherless America

A man entered a barber shop and noticed a young man sweeping the floor. The man struck up a conversation with the young fellow, who was shy and reserved. The man soon learned that the boy had no dad in his life.

"Son," the man asked, "who do you want to be like when you grow up?"

The boy shot back, "Mister, I ain't never met nobody that I want to be like when I grow up."

That story mirrors the situation an increasing number of children face. Warren Wiersbe made an observation that not only heightens the impact of this story, but adds a different twist that drives home its poignancy for contemporary dads and moms:

> We live in a world in which real heroes are scarce and we have to settle for substitutes, such as overrated movie stars and overpaid athletes and rock singers, people who are famous only for being

5

famous and, of course, for being rich. Even some of our favorite heroes of history have been reclassified by revisionist historians so that their achievements don't shine as gloriously as they once did. So, whether you're reading a history textbook, a new biography, or *Time*, you're probably finding it more and more difficult to discover somebody worthy of admiration, somebody you can call a hero or a heroine.[1]

TWO KEY QUESTIONS

I would like to ask two questions here of my fellow dads, one general and one specific:

1. Do you believe that at least one of every child's heroes should be his dad?

2. Do you genuinely want to be a hero to your child or children?

It may sound corny, but I want to be a hero to my three sons. I want to so impact my sons' lives for goodness and godliness that my influence on them will live on for generations.

Wade F. Horn is the director of the National Fatherhood Initiative. As the former U.S. Commissioner for Children and a child psychologist, he thought he was an expert on what made a good father. Yet when doctors diagnosed him with cancer six years ago, he realized with a jolt that he was closer to the first grade than graduate school in his expertise. He said, "It became clear to me in a personal way that if I were to have died because of that illness, my unfinished business would not have been in my clinical practice or in the federal bureaucracy. My unfinished business would have been my two little girls, who every morning when I was recuperating would come and give a kiss good-bye."[2]

Fortunately (or, perhaps for some fathers, unfortunately), most of us will not get a wake-up call of this nature. Nevertheless, I believe a wake-up call is far overdue for many dads who mean well and are trying to eke out a living and keep their children's heads above the cultural sea of crime, sex, and violence that is flooding our communities, schools, and homes.

ABSENCE MAKES THE SON GO WANDER

The cold, hard fact is that absentee fatherhood is becoming increasingly recognized as a strong (if not the leading) contributor to the cultural, moral, and spiritual meltdown of our nation. It is not saying too much to assert that children growing up without fathers is the number one social problem facing America today. Absenteeism, as Horn pointed out, is not confined to the inner city, nor is it caused solely by out-of-wedlock fathering. It is a phenomenon of the suburbs as well, with divorce and workaholism as the two primary culprits.[3]

Just how serious is this problem of fatherlessness? This statement drives it home with irresistible force: "Fatherlessness is the most harmful demographic trend of this generation. It is the leading cause of declining child well-being in our society. *It is also the engine driving our most urgent social problems*, from crime to adolescent pregnancy to child sexual abuse to domestic violence against women."[4]

Have a hard time believing this statement? Then consider the following startling fact. According to a study published in *The Journal of Research and Crime and Delinquency,* the best indicator of violent crime in a community is not race, income, or employment, but *the proportion of fatherless families.*[5]

Former U.S. Attorney General William Barr said, "If you look at the one factor that most closely correlates with crime, it's not poverty, it's not employment, it's not education; it's the absence of the father in the family."[6]

Dad, think of life as a series of snapshots that culminate in the big picture. Or, imagine life as a series of tests that lead to the final exam. In the best-selling book *Seven Habits of Highly Effective People*, Steven Covey identifies one of the seven habits as "Begin with the End in Mind."[7] As we begin this journey into a fresh look at fatherhood from a uniquely biblical perspective, I want you to begin to visualize—no, make that "visionize"—the man you want your boy (or the woman you want your daughter) to become. This is especially important if you are the father of sons, as I am. Consider these heart-breaking facts:

- Walk into a prison, and go to death row. Ninety-nine percent of those inmates are men. Go into the general population of that same prison, and 95 percent of those who fill the bunks are men.

- If you come upon the carnage caused by a drunken driver, you will see the footprints of a man 91 percent of the time.

- Come up on any traffic accident, and 75 percent of the time men are responsible.

- Thumb through all law enforcements' wanted posters looking for known drug dealers, and 98 percent of the time you will be looking at a man's face.

- Line up those who are responsible for child and spouse abuse cases, and you will find that 90 percent of the time it will be a man.[8]

Now I hope you see why it is every father's role, right, and responsibility to *help the boy to sit down and the man to stand up*—but more than this, to help him stand in a way that he, in turn, can help his children to stand as well. The same is true for daughters. I believe it was Dwight L. Moody who said, "If you want to know what kind of father you were, don't look at your children; look at your grandchildren."

IT TAKES LEADERSHIP

Dad, it takes *leadership* to do this. One of the greatest statements (and truest) I have ever heard is this one: "Everything rises and falls on leadership." I have seen that proven time and time again in practically every area of my life. It is especially true in the area of fatherhood.

Leadership involves at least three elements. First, *a leader must be willing to get out in front.* A leader must want to lead. If others sense the desire to lead is not present, their desire to follow will be absent. I will always believe that one of the major reasons George Bush lost to Bill Clinton in the 1992 U.S. presidential race is that the American people did not sense a "fire in the belly" in Bush to be president any longer. Dad, you must be willing to pay the price if you are going to be the leader of your family—and you will pay a higher price if you are not.

Second, *you must know where you are headed*. You must know where you want to lead others. No one wants to follow a leader who has no idea where he is going. I have a goal in mind as I am writing this book on fatherhood: to give our children a resource that will enable them to make wise decisions in the crucial areas of life. Sex, money, relationships, marriage, and vocation can make or break one's success in life. Dad, it is your job to teach your children, both in practice and precept, what those crucial life issues are and to help them to make godly decisions in each one.

The third element of leadership is *being there*. A leader must be around if he is going to lead. The problem with absentee fatherhood is absentee leadership. Allow me to give you my definition of a dad. I'll use an acrostic:

Direction
Availability
Discipline
Spirituality

The one crucial component in the above list is *availability*. Don't be misled: If you are not available, you cannot give direction, your discipline will be resented, and your spiritual leadership will be rejected.

Let me substitute one word in the above acrostic and watch what happens:

Direction
Unavailability
Discipline
Spirituality

The difference between a *dad* and a *dud* is simple: the difference between availability and unavailability. Men, especially grown men who are fathers, are a make-it or break-it factor in society. Listen to a prophecy from Daniel Patrick Moynihan, now a senator from

9

New York but in 1965 a young aide to Lyndon Johnson. Thirty years ago he penned these words:

> From the wild Irish slums of the nineteenth-century Eastern Seaboard to the riot-torn suburbs of Los Angeles, there is one unmistakable lesson in American history: a community that allows a large number of young men to grow up in broken families, dominated by women, never acquiring any stable relationship to male authority, never acquiring any set of rational expectations about the future—that community asks for and gets chaos. Crime, violence, unrest, unrestrained lashing out at the whole social structure—that is not only to be expected, it is very near inevitable.[9]

Since Moynihan penned those words, we have gone, in just two generations, from "Father Knows Best" to "Father Knows Less" to "Where Is Father?" What I am trying to say is this: *There is a great difference between fathering a child and being a father to a child.*

We live in a generation that, for the first time in American history, has failed to understand this. The most endangered species in America is not the spotted owl nor the snail darter, but the responsible father. More children will go to sleep tonight in a fatherless home than ever before in our nation's history. Consider the following:

- In 1960, fewer than six million children lived in single parent families. Today, the number is eighteen million.

- Almost 40 percent of American children live in a home in which their biological father is absent.

- Before they reach the age of eighteen, more than half of our nation's children are likely to spend at least a significant portion of their childhoods living apart from their fathers.

- For the first time in American history, the average child will live for a significant period of time without a father at home.[10]

FATHERLESSNESS: IT'S A CRYING SHAME

The devastation fatherlessness leaves in its wake is staggering. Think about the *emotional* devastation of fatherlessness:

- Fatherless children are anywhere from 100 to 200 percent more likely to have emotional and behavioral problems.

- A child who comes from a fatherless home is twice as likely to use drugs or alcohol, far more likely to become sexually active at an early age, and three times as likely to commit a violent crime.[11]

- Over 50 percent of teenagers who attempt suicide live in single family homes.

- Most runaways leave homes that are fatherless.

- Fatherless son are 300 percent more likely to become incarcerated in state juvenile institutions. Seventy percent of juveniles in long-term correctional facilities grew up without a father in the home.

- Fatherless daughters are 53 percent more likely to marry as teenagers, 111 percent more likely to have children as teenagers, 164 percent more likely to have an out-of-wedlock birth.

- Fatherless daughters who marry have a 92 percent higher divorce rate, and fatherless sons are 35 percent more likely to experience marital failure.[12]

- Eighty percent of teenagers admitted to psychiatric hospitals come from fatherless homes.[13]

Then there is the *intellectual* devastation. Children who come from fatherless homes:

- Display more antisocial behavior.

- Are 50 percent more likely to have learning disabilities.

11

- Do worse in school and are three times as likely to drop out as children who grow up in a home with a father.[14]

- Only 11.6 percent of children living with both parents repeat a grade in school. But for children of never married mothers, the number is 29.7 percent; and for children living with a divorced mother, it is 21.5 percent.[15]

Finally there is the *physical* devastation. Children who come from broken families where the father is absent are twenty to forty times more likely to suffer health problems than children who live with both parents.

LEAD, DON'T FOLLOW; AND DON'T GET OUT OF THE WAY

Fellow fathers, we must not forget that nature abhors a vacuum. If you don't lead your children, someone else will lead them for you. If you are not there for your children, someone else will be there for them—someone you may not like. When that happens, the greater problem is not that you won't be around, but that you will no longer be missed!

Four-year-old Tommy got a puppy on his birthday. He named it "Laddie," and he and the pup immediately became fast friends.

Unfortunately, the pup proved to be completely unmanageable. He refused to be housebroken, disobeyed every order, and seemed to enjoy destroying stockings, slippers, carpets, and furniture. The mother finally ran out of patience and shipped the dog to relatives far out in the country.

She was a bit leery about breaking the news to young Tommy, and so she waited until he was having his breakfast. Speaking softly, she said, "I sent Laddie away so you won't ever see him again."

To her surprised relief Tommy said, "No big deal, Mom. Don't worry about it," and he went out to play.

In a few minutes he came running back in, sobbing uncontrollably and almost hysterical. "Laddie's gone! Where's my dog? I want my dog!" he wailed.

"Son," his mother replied, "I told you at the breakfast table that Laddie was gone, and you seemed just fine. What's the problem?"

"Laddie?" the boy answered. "I thought you said 'Daddy'!"

There is an old saying that "You can't miss what you never had." I can't think of anything more tragic than to have your own children not even notice when you are gone. After I have been out of town for an extended period of time, one of the first things I ask my wife is, "Did the boys miss me?" If the day ever comes that she says no, my traveling days are over.

The day before I was writing these paragraphs, I went with my youngest son, Joshua, to Six Flags over Georgia, along with his fourth-grade class. I dutifully tagged along as he rode several rides with one of his classmates, who had been accompanied by his mother. We struck up a conversation, and I discovered that she and her son had recently joined our church.

When I asked if her husband was also a member, she said the only time he had attended our church was when she and her son had been baptized. She then began to open her soul and bare the heartache caused by her workaholic, absentee father-husband. "He is a good man, but he doesn't even see the need to accompany our son on things like this. I run my own business, and he could not understand why I would miss a day of making money just to waste a day at Six Flags with my son."

She then added an observation that crushed me—both for the son and the father. "Pastor, my son is so accustomed now to the fact that his dad does not spend time with him, he didn't even bother to ask him to come."

My son's class left the park early, but I stayed another three hours until the park closed, to be alone with my boy. I will never forget as we were walking out of the park—covered in white sugar, the remnants of a shared funnel cake—Joshua stopped me, gave me a big hug, and said, "Dad, thanks for taking me to Six Flags. You are my very best friend."

That, dads, can't be bought for money, marbles, or chocolate!

WHERE IS DAD?

May I share with you a radical thought? We live in a day when kids have never been given more of the things they want and less of the things they need. If you want an eye-opener, just go to your local mall, find a comfortable seat, and watch the kids and teenagers walk by. You will see everything from Madonna imitators to Dennis Rodman wanna-bes. Spiked hair, colored hair, dirty hair, carved hair, earrings, makeup, tattoos, spiked collars, and nose rings is *de rigueur*—and I am talking about the boys! I wonder, *Where is dad?*

Every time I see these kids driving their own cars, listening to their CDs on a state-of-the-art sound system, wearing their name-brand clothes, and strung out on drugs or alcohol they bought with somebody's money (their parents?), I wonder which is true: Do they not have a dad? Or do they have an absentee dad who doesn't care?

I would like to ask all of my fellow dads a question: Do you love your kids? Before you give a flippant, perhaps indignant yes, ponder this thought: *Love is not spelled t-h-i-n-g-s; it is spelled t-i-m-e.* Your kids need *you* more than they need the trinkets, treasures, and toys you can buy them (incidentally, that is also true for your wife).

Now, some of you dads may be tempted to pat yourself on the back as you observe that at least you *do* have the same address as your family. You may be tempted to think that just coming home every night after work gets you off the hook. Well, think again.

Fathers can be physically present, yet emotionally absent. In a 1990 *Los Angeles Times* poll, 57 percent of fathers said they feel guilty about spending too little time with their children. According to the Family Research Council, the average father spends only eight minutes a day in direct conversation with his children. In families where the mother works, too, it drops to four minutes.[16]

I realize most men who pick up this book are not in the category of fathers who are literally "missing in action." Yet there are many of us who are not truly taking the time to be the father our children need us to be. I hope to impress upon us all not only the importance of spending time with them, but also making the most of it when we do.

We can't afford to be like one golfer who was walking around the fairway with four caddies. A friend asked, "Why do you have so many caddies?"

"It's my wife's idea," the golfer answered. "She thinks I should spend more time with my kids."

What's happening in today's families is no joke, however. David Blankenhorn has observed that, over the past two hundred years, fatherhood has lost, in full or in part, each of its four traditional roles: irreplaceable caregiver, moral educator, head of family, and family breadwinner.[17] As one historian put it, "An eighteenth-century father would not recognize the distance contemporary men face between work and home . . . or the parental leadership granted to mothers or indeed the number of bad fathers."[18]

For proof, just listen to these unsettling words in a *Newsweek* column titled, "Dear Dads, Save Your Sons," by Christopher Bacorn, a psychologist living in Boerne, Texas. He tells about an anxious mother in her mid-thirties who came to his office with her fifteen-year-old son. The boy's dad had left four years before, and since then the teenager had descended into alcohol, gang membership, and violence. The mother had nowhere else to turn, and it was obvious the boy was at best a hostile participant. After attempting for thirty minutes to crack the steel vault of this boy's heart, Dr. Bacorn realized the futility of it all. He wrote these poignant and sad words:

> I have come to believe that most adolescent boys can't make use of professional counseling. . . . What a boy can use, and all too often doesn't have, is the fellowship of men—at least one man who pays attention to him, who spends time with him, and admires him. A boy needs a man he can look up to. What he doesn't need is a shrink. . . . As a nation, we are racked by youth violence, overrun by gangs, guns, and drugs. The great majority of youthful offenders are male, most without fathers *involved in their lives in any useful way.* Many have never even met their fathers.

15

What's become of the fathers of these boys? Where are they? Well, I can tell you where they are not. They're not at PTA meetings or piano recitals. They're not teaching Sunday school. You won't find them in the pediatrician's office, holding a sick child .
. . .

Where are the fathers? They are in diners and taverns, drinking, conversing, playing pool with other men. They are on golf courses, tennis courts, in bowling alleys, fishing on lakes and rivers. They are working in their jobs, many from early morning to late at night. Some are home watching television, out mowing the lawn or tuning up the car. In short, they are everywhere except in the company of their children.[19]

The father really is indispensable to "helping the boy (or girl) to sit down and the man (or woman) to stand up." There is a huge difference between biological reproduction and true fatherhood. One produces a child; the other produces an adult. Fatherlessness, the absence of paternal transmission—whether by physical absence or noninvolvement—inevitably contributes to a decline of character and competence in children.[20]

THE WINDOW CLOSES QUICKLY

Take it from someone who has seen the blur of infancy turn into the flash of adolescence and morph into the maelstrom of teenage life: The window of opportunity you have with your kids is not open wide, and it closes at supersonic speed. Your kids want your time and as much of it as they can get. I recently read a poem titled, "To My Grown-Up Son." I warn you, have your handkerchief out and ready—and take a deep breath before you read it.

My hands were busy through the day.
I didn't have much time to play
The little games you asked me to.
I didn't have much time for you.

16

I'd wash your clothes, I'd sew and cook,
But when you'd bring your picture book
And ask me please to share your fun,
I'd say, "A little later, son."
I'd tuck you in all safe at night
And hear your prayers, turn out the light,
Then tiptoe softly to the door.
I wish I'd stayed a minute more.
For life is short, the years rush past.
A little boy grows up so fast.
No longer is he at your side,
His precious secrets to confide
The picture books are put away,
There are no longer games to play,
No good-night kiss, no prayers to hear.
That all belongs to yesteryear.
My hands, once busy, now are still.
The days are long and hard to fill.
I wish I could go back and do
The little things you asked me to.[21]

Blankenhorn says something else in his book that alone is worth the price of the book. He says every man in the United States should be requested to take the following pledge:

> Many people today believe that fathers are unnecessary. I believe the opposite. I pledge to live my life according to the principle that every child deserves a father; that marriage is the pathway to effective fatherhood; that part of being a good man is being a good father; and that America needs more good men.[22]

As I bring this chapter to a close, pause for a moment and ask yourself this question: Is there a dad in *my* house? As a busy pastor of a large church, I often have to ask myself that question—and sometimes I do not like the answer.

17

Dad, you and I are needed and necessary in the lives of our sons and daughters. It is my prayer that the next few chapters will not only motivate you to invest your life in those you have brought into this world, but help you practically to arm them with godly wisdom that they might be victorious in the battle of everyday living.

I do not want merely to curse the darkness; I want to light a candle—no, make that a fire—in the heart of every father who picks up this book, to help us all be the dads our kids deserve. Dad, would you put this book down for a moment and join me in making the above pledge right now? Would you ask for God's help in making you not only a good father, but a godly father? Then would you pray that God would use the rest of this book to help us all to be better fathers? I join you in that prayer, and I trust the rest of this book will help us all be dads who make a difference.

Chapter 2

IF I HAD ONLY ONE WISH

*Fathers and mothers have lost the idea that
the highest aspiration they might have for
their children is for them to be wise. . . .
Specialized competence and success are all
that they can imagine.*

—Allan Bloom,
The Closing of the American Mind

One of my all-time favorite stories is "Aladdin and the Magic Lamp" in *The Arabian Knights*. As you remember, Aladdin finds a magic lamp that, when rubbed, produces a genie with the power to grant Aladdin's every wish.

We have all imagined finding such a lamp and making wishes that come true, so let me ask you a fun question: If you found such a lamp and you could have only one wish, what would you wish for? A humorous story illustrates that wise wishing requires a great deal of thought.

Three men were marooned on a desert island with no hope of rescue. One day they were walking around the island when one of them kicked up a lamp. He rubbed it; a genie appeared and offered each man one wish.

The first man excitedly said, "I wish I was back in my office in Boston." Poof! He was gone.

The second man said, "I wish I was at home with my family." Poof! He was gone.

The last man looked around and said, "It's so lonely here; I wish my friends were back with me."

Normally, wishing is like sitting in a rocking chair on the front porch on a windy day. It is a fun thing to do, but it won't get you anywhere. The problem with wishing is that genies and magic lamps simply do not exist—*but God does.* Since God does exist and He is more powerful than any genie, any wish in His will can become a reality. In fact, one time a wish did!

A WISE WISH

God gave to King Solomon the opportunity not only of a lifetime, but of an eternity. He did something for Solomon that, as far as the Bible reveals, He had never done before and never did again. He asked Solomon the most amazing question an omnipotent, infinite God can ask a weak, finite man.

"On that night God appeared to Solomon, and said to him, 'Ask! What shall I give you?'" (2 Chron. 1:7). Let that sink in for a moment. The Creator God said to a created man, "Your wish is my command." Solomon was given *carte blanche* by the One in whose dictionary the word *impossible* does not exist.

We need to understand this was more than only a privilege for Solomon; it was a test. At the tender age of twenty, King Solomon was about to find out who he was in the deepest core of his soul. An anonymous thinker wrote these words:

> Tell me your dreams, and I will read the riddle of your life. Tell me your prayers, and I will write the history of your soul. Tell me your askings, and I will tell you your gettings. Tell me what you seek, and I will tell you what you are. . . . I do not wish to know your possessions . . . only your wants. I do not care to know what you have, only what you have not

and desire to have; not your attainments, but what
you have not yet attained and follow after; that
which comes to you in your victories by day and
your dreams by night, the ideal you set before you,
the things you approve as excellent, what you seek
after and have given your heart to, these are the measure of a man.[1]

An egotistical person would have asked for fame. A materialis-
tic person would have asked for wealth. An ambitious person would
have asked for power. I dare say only one out of a billion people
would have asked for something outside of one of those three categories—but not Solomon. How does Solomon fill in the
blank?—with *wisdom.* "Now give me wisdom" (2 Chron. 1:10).

God granted Solomon's wish and gave him something more
valuable than wealth, more satisfying than fame, and more exhilarat-
ing than power. Indeed, all of these other things became a by-prod-
uct of the gift of wisdom.

God went on to promise Solomon, "Because this was in your
heart, and you have not asked riches or wealth or honor or the life of
your enemies, nor have you asked long life—but have asked wisdom
and knowledge for yourself, that you may judge My people over
whom I have made you king—wisdom and knowledge are granted to
you; and I will give you riches and wealth and honor, such as none of
the kings have had who were before you, nor shall any after you have
the like" (2 Chron. 1:11–12).

Did God keep His word? Well, consider this. What would you
have if you crossed an Arab sheik, the president of the United States,
Socrates, and Mickey Mouse? You would have the richest, most
powerful, wisest, and most famous person in the world—an apt
description of King Solomon in his day. Consider:

- He became the chief executive officer of the world's greatest
  empire.

- By his trading skills, he was acclaimed as the world's fore-
  most merchant.

21

- As the leading shipping magnate, he had a fleet of merchant ships that sailed throughout the world, collecting treasures.

- By his wealth he easily topped the Forbes 400 list.

- He was a master builder who constructed mammoth projects.

- His architectural designs became the world's most important buildings.

- He built vineyards, gardens, parks, and reservoirs.

- Tired of commerce, he turned to science, relentlessly pursuing the classification of nature.

- He was the chairman of the Joint Chiefs of Staff, building a vast army to defend and conquer.

- He was unanimously elected president of his country.

- He became the poet laureate of his nation.

- He had a distinguished career as a writer.

- He was a singularly gifted musician.[2]

Solomon learned the incredible worth of wisdom, enjoyed her benefits, and so wrote, "Wisdom is better than rubies, and all the things one may desire cannot be compared with her" (Prov. 8:11).

GOD'S TREASURE CHEST OF WISDOM

This background brings us to the Book of Proverbs. Proverbs is a treasure chest containing the nuggets of wisdom which Solomon mined from the heart of God. When you study Proverbs, you strike the mother lode of heavenly wisdom for earthly living. But dad, *Proverbs is far more than that.*

For more than ten years now I have read one chapter in the Book of Proverbs every day. Why? Because I want wisdom—not the counterfeit, pseudo-intellectual knowledge this world manufactures, but wisdom poured straight out of the bucket of God's heart.

For years I came to this river of wisdom, panning each day for some golden nugget of heavenly brilliance that I could stash away in my pouch of daily living. I never gave much thought either to the One who had buried these nuggets beneath the ground of Holy Scripture or why He even bothered. Then I made an amazing discovery.

As I was reading Proverbs one morning, two words suddenly leaped off the page. I had never noticed them before. The words were, *my son*. I hurriedly ran to my computer and pulled up the phrase on my concordance. This is what I saw:

> *My son*, hear the instruction of your father,
> And do not forsake the law of your mother. (1:8)

> *My son*, if sinners entice you,
> Do not consent. (1:10)

> *My son*, do not walk in the way with them,
> Keep your foot from their path. (1:15)

> *My son*, do not forget my law,
> But let your heart keep my commands. (3:1)

> *My son*, do not despise the chastening of the LORD,
> Nor detest His correction. (3:11)

> *My son*, let them not depart from your eyes—
> Keep sound wisdom and discretion. (3:21)

> Hear, *my son*, and receive my sayings,
> And the years of your life will be many. (4:10)

> *My son*, pay attention to my wisdom;
> Lend your ear to my understanding. (5:1)

> For why should you, *my son*,
>   be enraptured by an immoral woman,
> And be embraced in the arms of a seductress? (5:20)

23

My son, if you become surety for your friend,
If you have shaken hands in pledge for a stranger.
(6:1)

So do this, *my son*, and deliver yourself;
For you have come into the hand of your friend:
Go and humble yourself;
Plead with your friend. (6:3)

My son, keep your father's command,
And do not forsake the law of your mother. (6:20)

My son, keep my words,
And treasure my commands within you. (7:1)

Cease listening to instruction, *my son*,
And you will stray from the words of knowledge.
(19:27)

My son, if your heart is wise,
My heart will rejoice—indeed, I myself. (23:15)

Hear, *my son*, and be wise;
And guide your heart in the way. (23:19)

My son, give me your heart,
And let your eyes observe my ways. (23:26)

My son, eat honey because it is good,
And the honeycomb which is sweet to your taste.
(24:13)

My son, fear the LORD and the king;
Do not associate with those given to change. (24:21)

My son, be wise, and make my heart glad,
That I may answer him who reproaches me. (27:11)

What, *my son?*
And what, son of my womb?
And what, son of my vows? (31:2)

Twenty-three times this phrase is used. In addition, the phrase "my children" is used four times (Prov. 4:1; 5:7; 7:24; 8:32). As I meditated on this startling discovery, suddenly the lights came on—Proverbs is not just a book; it is a letter. But more than that, it is a letter from a father *to a son.*

Solomon did not sit down one day in the portico of his palace and, out of sheer boredom and with nothing else to do, say, "I think I'll write a book on wisdom and show how sharp I really am." Rather, I believe he came to realize that his greatest legacy was not his money, his fame, or his power, but his family.

Indeed, the theme of the book is captured in something Solomon's father, David, said to him many years before:

Wisdom is the principal thing;
Therefore get wisdom.
And in all your getting, get
understanding. (Prov. 4:7)

In short, Proverbs is more than a random collection of pithy maxims strung together willy-nilly; it is *godly wisdom passed down from a father to his children to enable them to maximize their potential for living a God-blessed, meaningful life.* In other words, Proverbs is a tool that a dad can use to help his children "wise up in a dumbing down world." When I saw this, I began to hear the heart of a father pulsate on every page.

Then my eyes were opened to still another unique twist to this "letter." This letter to a son is *from a father.* The book begins with this salutation: "My son, hear the instruction of your *father*" (1:8).[3] The word *father* is used nineteen times in Proverbs;[4] I believe this is another key that unlocks the meaning of this book. Proverbs is a letter *from* a father *about* fathers and *to* fathers. It not only teaches a father how to *lead* his children, but how to *live* before his children.

THE GIFT THAT LASTS

Dad, stop right here and nail this next statement to the door of your heart. *Wisdom is the one gift you can pass on to your children that will last beyond your lifetime.* You can leave your children money, but eventually they will spend it. You can leave your children property, but eventually they will sell it. You can leave your family trinkets and toys, but eventually they will either lose them or give them away. But when you leave them wisdom, your gift lasts forever!

Proverbs 4 is a revealing picture both of a precious memory in Solomon's mind and the purpose for Proverbs that was in Solomon's heart. First, he recalled his days as a young child when he was the apple of David's eye. Take in the picture he painted for us:

> Hear, my children, the instruction of a father,
> And give attention to know understanding;
> For I give you good doctrine:
> Do not forsake my law.
> When I was my father's son,
> Tender and the only one in the sight of my
>   mother,
> He also taught me, and said to me:
> "Let your heart retain my words;
> Keep my commands, and live." (Prov. 4:1–4)

We see that David was not only a king in a castle; he was a professor in his home. This passage reveals the centerpiece of the advice David gave to young Solomon. He drilled one thought into the heart and mind of Solomon early on:

> Get wisdom! Get understanding! . . .
> Wisdom is the principal thing;
> *Therefore* get wisdom.
> And in all your getting, get
>   understanding. (Prov. 4:5, 7)

Now, this was what happened to Solomon in the past, as a son. But Solomon wrote Proverbs in the present, as a father. He had moved from the role of student to teacher. So he said,

> Hear, my son, and receive my sayings,
> And the years of your life will be many.
> I have taught you in the way of wisdom;
> I have led you in right paths. (Prov. 4:10–11)

Dad, don't miss what Solomon said here. *He took the wisdom baton from his father and wanted to pass it on to his children.* What Solomon did, you can do, for you have the manual of wisdom in Proverbs. You can take the baton of wisdom from the heavenly Father and pass it down to your own children.

The fact that God placed Solomon's wisdom in His Word tells us that this was not human wisdom raised to a supernatural height, but supernatural wisdom lowered to human understanding. From the beginning, Solomon repeatedly encouraged fathers to dive into this ocean of wisdom and drink from its fountain of truth. Lest you think the water is too deep and wisdom is beyond you, listen first to what the wisest man in the world told us about wisdom.

WISDOM: YOU CAN FIND IT IF YOU SEEK IT

We are living in a world that is drowning in knowledge, yet starving for wisdom. It was a wise eye that made this salient observation:

> Since 1955 knowledge has doubled every five years; libraries groan with the weight of new books. . . . In fact, our generation possesses more data about the universe and human personality than all previous generations put together. High school graduates today have been exposed to more information about the world than Plato, Aristotle, Spinoza, or Benjamin Franklin. In terms of facts alone, neither Moses nor Paul could pass a college entrance exam today.

27

Yet, by everyone's standards, even with all our knowledge . . . society today is peopled with a bumper crop of brilliant failures. . . . men and women educated to earn a living often don't know anything about handling life itself. Alumni from noted universities have mastered information about a narrow slice of life, but couldn't make it out of the first grade when it comes to living successfully with family and friends. Let's face it. Knowledge is not enough to meet life's problems. We need wisdom, the ability to handle life with skill.[5]

If our generation has learned anything, it should have learned by now that knowledge is no substitute for wisdom. Charles Spurgeon once said, "Wisdom is the right use of knowledge. To know is not to be wise. Many men know a great deal and are all the greater fools for it. There is no fool so great a fool as a knowing fool; but to know how to use knowledge is to have wisdom."[6]

Well, I've got great news for all of us dads—the wisdom we need is abundantly available, and we can find it if we seek it! Solomon said in Proverbs 2:4–5,

If you seek her as silver,
And search for her as for hidden treasures;
Then you will understand the fear of the LORD,
And find the knowledge of God.

I repeat: Proverbs is God's treasure chest of heavenly wisdom. You don't have to look long to find it, and when you do find it you don't have to unlock it. All you have to do is open it and enjoy the jewels of wisdom that are there.

Solomon compares wisdom to a cry that can be heard anywhere (1:20–21) and to a free meal that can be eaten at any time (9:1–6). So dad, understand up front—whether or not you avail yourself of God's wisdom, God's wisdom is available.

28

WISDOM: YOU CAN HAVE IT IF YOU WANT IT

Solomon goes on to say, "Yes, if you cry out for discernment, and lift up your voice for understanding" (Prov. 2:3). In other words, if you ask for wisdom, you will get wisdom. I want to give to every dad a fail-safe, foolproof formula for getting wisdom.

First, you must admit you need it. Benjamin Franklin rightly said, "The doorstep to the temple of wisdom is a knowledge of your own ignorance."[7]

Second, you must go to the right source, and the only infallible source of wisdom is God. "For the LORD gives wisdom" (v. 6). Only God can give wisdom because only God has wisdom.

In fact, not only does God have a monopoly on wisdom, but His wisdom makes our wisdom look like foolishness. Paul said that even "the *foolishness* of God is wiser than man's wisdom" (1 Cor. 1:25, NIV). Now, think about that. If God were capable of a stupid thought (which, of course, He is not), that thought would be wiser than the wisest thought a human being could ever conceive.[8]

Fathers, listen up! The eternal Father knows more about how to raise children than all earthly fathers who have ever lived, put together. And God is not hoarding his wisdom; He is eager to give it away. "If any of you lacks wisdom, let him ask of God, who gives to all liberally and without reproach, and it will be given to him" (James 1:5). But you must ask for it. You fail to do so at your own peril.

You don't have to golf to appreciate the following true story. As you probably know, professional golfers play with a caddie. The caddie is more than a carrier of clubs; he is there for support and valuable advice.

Tommy Bolt was one of the greatest golfers of all time, but he had one major flaw, a volcanic temper. One year he was playing in a tournament in southern California, and he was still steaming because of a bad round the day before. He told his caddie only to say, "Yes, Mr. Bolt," or "No, Mr. Bolt," if he was asked a question. Otherwise, he was to keep silent.

Bolt hit his first tee shot, and it appeared to come to rest behind a tree. When they reached the spot, Bolt asked his caddie, "Do you think I should hit a five-iron?" The caddie, obeying orders, simply replied, "No, Mr. Bolt." Bolt hit the five-iron anyway and made an unbelievable shot that landed on the green a few feet from the hole.

He turned to his caddie and proudly said, "What did you think about that shot?"

As the caddie picked up the bag and headed toward the green, he simply said, "It wasn't your ball, Mr. Bolt."[9] Better to ask for wisdom now than to look foolish later!

WISDOM: YOU CAN USE IT WHEN YOU GET IT

Wisdom is not some aloof professor sitting in an ivory tower, oblivious to the needs of the people below. Real wisdom wears shoe leather, overalls, drives a pickup truck, goes to the grocery store, paints houses, draws a paycheck, suffers in the hospital, and cries at the funeral home. Remember, wisdom is to be found in "the open squares, . . . the chief concourses, . . . the gates in the city" (1:20–21). Wisdom gets down to the nitty-gritty of life. It is where the action is.

Since this book is about helping your children to make wise decisions, let me give you a working definition of wisdom: *Wisdom is seeing life through the eyes of God, and living life in the will of God.* Proverbs not only gives fathers the skills to be wise dads, but also enables them to pass along the skills of wisdom to their children.

Basically, Proverbs deals with the five major areas of life: the financial, the emotional, the physical, the relational, and the spiritual. I think all of us dads would agree that if we can help our children be wise in those five areas of life, we will have done a good life's work. The rest of this book gives us principles of godly wisdom to enable our children to be successful in these five areas.

THE RESULTS OF BAD ADVICE

One of commentator Paul Harvey's most requested and highly popular addresses is "They Gave Us Some Bad Advice." I would like to reproduce it here, for it reminds me of what knowledge without wisdom has done to our generation and how badly our children need wise fathers.

"They" told us if we'd relax about sex, take our clothes off, and not get all uptight about it, that there would be no more sex crimes.

So we let it all hang out—and the incidence of rape has increased 12% in one year!

Maybe we'd better question some of the other advice "they" have given us.

"They" told us we had been too tough with criminals; that we should go easy on them. So we went easy on them—and the rate of violent crime has increased 40% since 1983.

"They" told us to be more generous with poor folks. So we were. Now the Census Bureau says there are more "poor" than ever!

"They" said that churches were "old-fashioned," that they must modernize, liberalize, rationalize, compromise.

And those that compromise most are shrinking fastest.

If it is appearing up to here that "they" gave us some awfully bad advice, they did.

"They" insisted that our schools must boot od out and rely on enhancing Junior's intelligence.

So we graduated a generation of Juniors with refined intellects and undisciplined emotions—so school-age suicides have increased.

"They" told us alcoholism and drug addictions were sicknesses, not crimes. Now we are gagging, choking, strangling, on forbidden fruit.

"They" said informal marriage was enough, so now the odds are 5-to-4 your rapture will be ruptured and 2-in-7 that the next baby will be born illegitimate.

Who are these "they" who have been thus misleading us?

"They" are the materialists who deify the finite sciences.

"They" meant well, but their intentions are paving the road to hell.

Now, Paul Harvey, you've quit commentating and gone to preachin'. I don't mean to, but I can't separate goodness and badness from today's news and explain it.

Every ugly headline in today's newspaper—and yesterday's, and tomorrow's—is because somebody's emotions got out of whack.

He might be as smart as all get-out, but if he's emotionally color-blind he is an unguided missile destined inevitably to self-destruct.

Spaceship Earth came with a book of instructions; let's see what it says:

> It says we should not be slothful in business. In fact, it says, "He who does not work—let him not eat."
>
> It says women should wear modest apparel.
>
> It says don't steal anything—*any-thing!*
>
> It says don't get drunk—.
>
> It says you sleep only with your own wife.
>
> It says you don't do what you "want," you do what you "ought," and for those whose consciences are anesthetized, it specifies which is which.

In other words, if that rule book were not divinely inspired, it would still be the best blueprint for an orderly existence.

If it did not promise life hereafter, it would still contain the best formula for a good life here.[10]

My sentiments exactly! By the way, if I had only one wish it would be about the same as the wish of one great author, Chuck

Swindoll, who said, "If I could have only one wish for God's people, it would be that all of us would return to the Word of God, that we would realize once for all that His Book has the answers."[11]

My wish for all of us dads is that we would turn back to the one Book that has the answers for all the problems that our kids face, and be godly enough and wise enough to pass along these answers to our children. That is what I want for my children, and yours too.

Dad, would you right now put down this book and pray this simple prayer with me? It's a prayer that, if said sincerely, can have dramatic and positive effects on your family for generations to come:

> Lord, I need wisdom; wisdom to be the dad to my children that I know You want me to be. I humbly admit my own ignorance, and I confidently ask that You would keep Your Word and, on a daily basis, give me the divine wisdom to be the kind of dad that I need to be. I pledge, with Your help, to pass godly wisdom down onto my children, and I thank You for hearing my prayer. In Jesus' name, Amen.

PART 2

WISING UP
IN A DUMBING DOWN
WORLD

Chapter 3

PUT UP AND SHUT UP

I have never been hurt by anything I didn't say.

—Calvin Coolidge

t's a funny thing with kids: After they are born, we can hardly wait until they start talking; then after they learn to talk, we can hardly wait for them to shut up! Someone has observed that children go through four stages in their communication with their fathers. First, they call us "Da-da." Then they call us "Daddy." Then they call us "Dad." Then they call us "collect!"

Solomon was extremely concerned that his children be wise in the way they used their tongues. He made this strong statement about that little critter that lies behind our teeth: "Death and life are in the power of the tongue, and those who love it will eat its fruit" (Prov. 18:21).

Almost one hundred years ago the following statement was made, and it is as true today: "There is nothing which seems more insubstantial than speech, a mere vibration in the atmosphere which touches the nerves of hearing and then dies away. There is no organ which seems smaller and less considerable than the tongue; a little member which is not even seen, and physically speaking, soft and weak. But the word which issues out of the lips is the greatest power in human life."[1]

Never underestimate the awesome power of the spoken word. For every word in Adolf Hitler's book, *Mein Kampf,* 125 people died in World War II.[2]

Only one man in the history of America ever resigned from the presidency: Richard Nixon. Have you ever considered what really brought Mr. Nixon down? Conventional thinking said it was the tapes of his private conversations. But it was not the tapes; it was his tongue. It was not the tapes, but *what he said on the tapes* that sealed his doom.

Solomon had much to say about what comes out of our mouths. In fact, the words *tongue, mouth, lips,* and *words* are mentioned in Proverbs almost 150 times, roughly five times in each of the thirty-one chapters.[3] The fact that Solomon placed so much emphasis on our words tells us that we had better take care of the sounds that flow from our mouths.

Consider this: In a lifetime of fifty years, the average person speaks enough to make twelve thousand volumes of three hundred pages each. If that is the average, think about the libraries many of us are leaving behind! (I know of one person who speaks 300 words a minute with gusts up to 750!) No wonder Solomon took so much time and poured so much thought into this vital topic.

IT DOESN'T TAKE MUCH TO SAY A LOT

Consider how even a small number of words will determine the fabric and destiny of the lives of your children:

- "I love you." These words can lead to engagement.

- "Will you marry me?" These words can lead to a lifetime commitment.

- "Let's start a family." These words can determine future children and grandchildren.

- "My major in college is going to be ———." These words can determine a lifetime vocation.

- "Yes." This word spoken to Jesus Christ can ensure an eternity with God.

- "No." This word spoken to Jesus Christ can ensure an eternity without God.

You have learned by now how badly Solomon wanted his children to be wise, but he gave us a specific reason why he desired a heart of wisdom for his children:

> My son, if your heart is wise,
> My heart will rejoice—indeed, I myself;
> Yes, my inmost being will rejoice
> When your lips speak right things.
>   (Prov. 23:15–16, italics mine)

With their hearts Solomon wanted his children to think wisely. With their hands Solomon wanted his children to do wisely. But with their lips Solomon wanted his children to speak wisely.

A little ditty I heard years ago perfectly summarizes what Solomon is telling our children:

> If your lips you would keep from slips,
> Five things observe with care:
> To whom you speak; of whom you speak;
> And how, and when, and where.[4]

Remember, dad, we are living in an age where saying the wrong thing can either get you sued or get you shot. You will be hard-pressed to find a greater life lesson to teach your children than how to control their tongues.

HOW WORDS CAN GIVE EMOTIONAL WHIPLASH

One verse especially encapsulates Solomon's overarching philosophy concerning human speech and the central lesson he wanted his children to learn: "He who guards his mouth preserves his life, but he who opens wide his lips shall have destruction" (Prov. 13:3). Put simply, the less we think, the more we speak, and the quicker we say it, the more likely we are to get into trouble.

Unfortunately, many times we get into the situation of the vacuum cleaner salesman who had been assigned an extremely back-woods, rural area for his territory. He was going from farmhouse to farmhouse on his first day on the job, trying to sell vacuum cleaners. As he approached one farmhouse, he knocked on the door and was met by a farmer's wife who asked him what he wanted.

Without even asking permission, he barged right past her into the kitchen and said, "I'm selling vacuum cleaners."

"Wait a minute," she replied.

"Ma'am, before you say anything, I want to show you something," he insisted.

"But—"

"Watch this!" he commanded as he reached into his bag, pulled out a bucket of dirt, and threw it all over her wooden floor. "If my vacuum cleaner won't pick all that dirt up," he boasted, "I'll eat it!"

She looked at the man and said, "Then you better get busy, 'cause we ain't got no electricity."

How often we have to eat the words we so carelessly throw about on the floor of everyday living!

Every time I think about this subject of the tongue, I am reminded of another story about a mother who was preparing dinner one evening when her little boy came running into the kitchen.

"What has Mama's little darling been doing all day?" she asked.

"I've been playing mailman," he replied.

"Mailman?" the mother wondered aloud. "How could you do that when you had no letters?"

"Oh, I had a whole bunch of letters."

"What letters?"

"I found them in the old trunk up in the attic all tied up with ribbon, and I put one in every mailbox on the street."

I want to remind you, dad, and you need to remind your kids: Every word that comes out of your mouth is put into God's mailbox.

We will be judged by every idle word we say. So teach your kids early, and teach your kids often:

> Be careful of the words you say
> And keep them soft and sweet;
> You never know from day to day
> Which ones you'll have to eat.

I guarantee you, if you can teach your children how to control their tongues, you'll substantially improve their diets.

VERBAL ARSON

Proverbs issues stern warnings to the gossip, to the loose cannon, to the person who indiscriminately goes about spreading rumors like wildfire. Solomon repeatedly warned his children about being involved in gossip, either on the giving end or on the receiving end. On the one hand, he warned about the one who gossips:

> A talebearer reveals secrets,
> But he who is of a faithful spirit
>   conceals a matter. (Prov. 11:13)

> A perverse man sows strife,
> And a whisperer separates the
>   best of friends. (Prov. 16:28)

The word *talebearer* comes from the Hebrew word *rakal* which literally means "to go about." It is probably derived from a word meaning "merchant."[5] A talebearer is someone who goes about peddling gossip!

I define *gossip* as "a false or unverified report concerning another person discussed with a third party in a negative fashion with the intent to do verbal harm." Gossip is damaged goods sold at a premium price, spoiling both the seller and the buyer.

41

I read something that struck me as a great lesson all of us dads could teach our kids. Here it is: People cannot be judged by what others say about them, but they can be judged by what they say about others.

While preparing this chapter I read about an interesting creature called the ant lion, more popularly known as the "doodlebug." The doodlebug lives at the bottom of a little cone-shaped hole he burrows in the sand.

He gets down as low as possible into that cone so he's always looking up to everything else. When an ant comes around and gets on the side of this carefully prepared cone, the doodlebug feels a few grains of sand slide down, which signals him that food is up there. Then the doodlebug begins to throw dirt on his victim. What he is trying to do is drag that ant down to his level. This is exactly what we do when we gossip—we throw dirt on others, hoping to bring them down to our level.

That is why Solomon warned not only against being a gossip-bearer, but also a gossip-hearer. This lesson is so important that he repeated a proverb word for word in two places in his book, something he did only rarely. Proverbs 18:8 and 26:22 are identical: "The words of a talebearer are like tasty trifles, and they go down into the inmost body."

The ear craves gossip like a hungry stomach craves food. That's why Solomon goes on to give this warning: "He who goes about as a talebearer reveals secrets; therefore do not associate with one who flatters with his lips" (Prov. 20:19). Your kids will have one of two tendencies: either to have gossipy lips or gossipy ears. If they have gossipy lips, teach them not to share gossip. If they have gossipy ears, teach them not to receive it.

In most states it is illegal both to steal and to receive stolen goods. That is why the apostle Paul admonished, "Do not *receive* an accusation against an elder except from two or three witnesses" (1 Tim. 5:19). Remember, the gossiper must always have an accomplice to commit the crime!

WITH WORDS "THE MORE THE SADDER"

"In the multitude of words sin is not lacking, but he who restrains his lips is wise" (Prov. 10:19). This is not only a law of speech, but a law of science. I think it can be proven that your odds of putting your foot in your mouth increase exponentially the more times you open it. Put another way, the potential for saying the wrong thing increases proportionately to the number of words you say. (That is why the longer the sermon, the more prepared and prayed up the preacher had better be!)

Have you ever noticed that the person who is always putting in his two cents worth usually says something that is worth about two cents? I read something recently that gave me pause. It said, "He who thinks by the inch and speaks by the yard should be kicked by the foot." I could put it this way: "When you open your lips, don't shoot from the hips or you'll shoot yourself in the behind."

Only a fool speaks rashly and recklessly. Indeed, a person who is hasty in his words is worse than a fool. Solomon recorded this sage observation: "Do you see a man hasty in his words? There is more hope for a fool than for him" (Prov. 29:20). When it comes to our words, "haste makes waste."

It is like the man who walked into a bird shop one day. A parrot was sitting on a perch, and in quite a cocky fashion the man looked at the parrot and said, "Hey, stupid, can you speak?" To the man's surprise the parrot replied, "Yes, dummy, can you fly?"

Solomon never forgot his own advice, even as an old man. In Ecclesiastes 5:2 he wrote,

> Do not be rash with your mouth,
> And let not your heart utter
>   anything hastily before God.
> For God is in heaven, and you on earth;
> Therefore let your words be few.

A humorous story reminds me how it behooves us all to speak less and listen more. There was a wealthy grandfather who was getting up in age. Because he was going deaf he went to the doctor and was fitted with a unique hearing aid. It not only overcame the old man's deafness and allowed him to hear perfectly, but it was concealed so no one could see it.

When he went back to the doctor for a checkup, the doctor said, "Your family must be extremely happy to know that you can now hear." The grandfather said, "Well, I haven't told them about my hearing aid. I just sit around and listen to the conversations. I've already changed my will three times."

SINCERITY IS THE BEST FORM OF FLATTERY

Young people are especially susceptible to flattery. I am convinced that most one-night stands and adulterous liaisons begin with a flattering comment. Listen to Eugene Peterson's unique translation of Proverbs 29:5: "A flattering neighbor is up to no good; he's probably planning to take advantage of you."[6] Flatterers will do you no good. In fact, Solomon says that, in the long run, you are better off with a man who will criticize you than a man who will flatter you. "He who rebukes a man will find more favor afterward than he who flatters with the tongue" (Prov. 28:23).

The English word *flatter* comes from a French term that means "to pat, smooth, or caress."[7] A flatterer is someone who will pat you on the back with one hand and knife you in the back with the other. Flattery is something a person will say to your face but will not say behind your back. It is insincere praise from an insincere motive.

We can teach our children two wonderful lessons about the fine line between praise and flattery (and the best way to teach them is to remember ourselves to keep from crossing that line):

> Lesson #1: Teach your children to give praise sparingly but sincerely, with nothing but the best in mind for the other person.
> Lesson #2: Teach your children to receive praise wisely, without taking either themselves or the person giving the praise too seriously.

Solomon wisely reminded his children "The crucible is for silver and the furnace for gold, and a man *is tested* by the praise accorded him" (Prov. 27:21, NASB). A question one should always ask of himself when he is praised is: Does this make me more bigheaded or more bighearted?

Never forget that flattery was the weapon the serpent used to sink Eve's ship in the garden of Eden.

KEEP IT CLEAN OR KEEP IT CLOSED!

I don't think I have to tell any father the problem our society has with profanity and foul language. I was in a mall recently and could hardly believe the language of kids who could not have been more than twelve or thirteen years of age. There is one thing we have never tolerated in our family, and never will, and that is foul language.

You can tell what kind of effect you are having on your children in their training and discipline by the words they use, especially when they get angry. Listen to these two statements, back to back:

> The heart of the righteous
> studies how to answer,
> But the mouth of the wicked
> pours forth evil. (Prov. 15:28)

> The lips of the righteous know
> what is acceptable,
> But the mouth of the wicked
> what is perverse. (Prov. 10:32)

The first statement tells us that a wise person will think before he speaks because he realizes every word has a consequence. The second verse tells us that the lips of a righteous person automatically know what is acceptable to say and keeps in mind that God hears every word.

When George Bush was running for president in 1988, he admitted that he had made inappropriate remarks about Dan Rather and CBS White House correspondent Leslie Stall after an on-the-air confrontation. Bush referred to Rather in an unprintable term and also took God's name in vain in speaking about CBS.

When confronted with what he had said, he replied, "If I had known the microphone was on I would not have taken the Lord's name in vain, and I apologize for that. I didn't know I was being taped, or I wouldn't have done it."[8] The fact is, the president shouldn't have said it whether the tape was running or not. Remember, God's tape is always running. "The ways of man are before the eyes of the LORD, and He ponders all his paths" (Prov. 5:21). Centuries later Jesus Himself declared, "There is nothing concealed that will not be disclosed, or hidden that will not be made known. What you have said in the dark will be heard in the daylight, and what you have whispered in the ear in the inner rooms will be proclaimed from the roofs" (Luke 12:2–3, NIV).

Dad, I urge you, be firm with your children and never allow them to use profane or filthy language. And I implore you to set the example by the kind of language you use. I've never done a scientific study, but I'm certain you'd find 98 percent of the teenagers and young people who use foul language heard it first at home.

THERE'S GOLD IN THEM THAR TONGUES!

Solomon compared wise words, spoken in a timely fashion, to gold and silver.

> A word fitly spoken is like
>   apples of gold
> In settings of silver.
> Like an earring of gold and an
>   ornament of fine gold
> Is a wise rebuker to an obedient ear.
>   (Prov. 25:11–12)

One mark of wisdom is the ability to say the right thing, in the right way, at the right time, to the right person—or not to say anything at all. One saying not found in the Book of Proverbs still contains powerful truth: "As a man grows wiser he talks less and says more."

Keep in mind that the key to the tongue is the heart. That is why Solomon said in Proverbs 18:4, "The words of a man's mouth are deep waters; the wellspring of wisdom is a flowing brook." "Deep waters" refers to the water at the bottom of the well that is the cleanest and the coldest.

If you want to know what kind of water a well really has, go down to the bottom to get it. If you want to know what is in a person's heart, listen to his or her words. As the old country farmer put it, "What is down in the well comes up in the bucket."

The mouth is like an overflow pipe. It not only reveals what is in the heart but what *fills* the heart. Every time we speak, we raise the curtain of our hearts, exposing what it is really like.[9] Again, one of the benefits of instilling wisdom early on in the heart of your children is the purifying and sanctifying effect it has on their words.

As my children began to hear the wrong kinds of words at school, they brought them home, usually in the form of a question: "Daddy, what does ——— mean?" I always answered the question with another question: "Have you ever heard daddy use this word?" Of course, the answer was no. I then proceeded to tell them not only why that word was inappropriate, but how God hears every word we say and holds us accountable for all of them.

I will never forget one time when our family was out and we heard a profane word used by a nearby man. I believe it was Jonathan who said, "*We* don't talk like that, do *we*, Daddy?" Sweet words about dirty words, wouldn't you say?

Our instruction to our children must continuously be to their hearts as well as to their heads. When their hearts are right, what they speak will be right. The tongue is not only a barometer of physical health, but also of spiritual health. We can glean three life lessons to teach our children about the wise use of their tongues.

1. USE THE TONGUE CAUTIOUSLY

One of the most groundbreaking, far-reaching judicial opinions ever handed down by the Supreme Court was the *Miranda* decision.

That opinion determined that every criminal suspect had a constitutional right to be advised of the availability of counsel. Part of what police are required to tell suspects under *Miranda* reads, "You have the right to remain silent. Anything you say can, and will, be used against you."

We ought to exercise that right far more often in everyday living than we normally do. Sometimes the wisest words are the ones never spoken. I don't know who said this, but I agree with it: "A wise man is one who thinks twice before saying nothing."

Say, would you like for people to think you are smarter than you really are, rather than discover that you are dumber than they thought you were? Let me tell you a secret:

> He who has knowledge spares his words,
> And a man of understanding is of a calm spirit.
> Even a fool is counted wise
>   when he holds his peace;
> When he shuts his lips, he is
>   considered perceptive. (Prov. 17:27–28)

It is better to keep your mouth shut and let people think you are a fool, than to open it and remove all doubt! I have learned, the hard way, that one minute of keeping my mouth shut is worth an hour of explanation.

My first job as a teenager was in a local department store called "Dixie City." The manager was a Jewish man whose last name was Grooh. I made up a little ditty about "Grooh the Jew," and unbeknownst to me, it was overheard by Mr. Grooh himself.

He was a kind gentleman, and rather than fire me, he let it slide. Another employee, however, saw what had happened and told me that Mr. Grooh had indeed overheard me singing my stupid little song.

It was hard, but I did the right thing. I went into his office, confessed, and asked his forgiveness. But I could tell from the look on his face that irreparable damage had been done and my Christian witness had been tarnished. I learned too late that when in doubt say nothing, for it sure beats saying the wrong something!

One of the most underrated presidents of all time, in my opinion, was Calvin Coolidge. He was known as "Silent Cal" because he spoke very little. Yet he said one of the wisest things, without saying anything, that I've heard anybody say about anything. It is the quote heading up this chapter: "I have never been hurt by anything I didn't say."

This is not from the *Miranda* decision, but you could call it the *Merritt Manifesto:* "What you *don't* say *can't* and *won't* be used against you." Obviously, you may be misquoted or falsely quoted, but it is better to have others try to prove you said something you did not say than to condemn you for something you did say.

2. USE THE TONGUE CAREFULLY

Solomon not only condemns the tongue that starts gossip; he also praises the tongue that stops gossip.

> A talebearer reveals secrets,
> But he who is of a faithful spirit
>   conceals a matter. (Prov. 11:13)

> He who covers a transgression seeks love,
> But he who repeats a matter separates friends.
>   (Prov. 17:9)

The tongue should be used as a gossip-stopper, not a gossip-starter. Teach your children to ask four questions of anyone who wants to tell them a juicy piece of information about someone else. These are guaranteed gossip-stoppers:

- How do you know this is true? (If its truth cannot be verified, it should not be reported.)

- Is this confidential? (If it is, the conversation is over.)

- Is it kind? (If it is not, why is the person sharing it?)

- Is it necessary? (If it is not, then talk about something else.)

3. USE THE TONGUE CONSTRUCTIVELY

There is no greater word that one can hear or speak than an encouraging word. Solomon said, "Anxiety in the heart of man causes depression, but a good word makes it glad" (Prov. 12:25). I have learned how vitally important encouragement is in the life of a family. Encouragement is like a peanut butter sandwich—the more you spread it around, the better things stick together.

My oldest son, James, played one year of little league ball when he was six years old. The entire season he did not as much as touch the ball in one at bat—not even a foul tip! But what he carries with him to this day is the fact that I was always encouraging him, telling him how proud I was that he was standing up at the plate to face the pitchers with those twenty-mile-per-hour hummers coming at him. Not once did I yell, scream, or berate him for being the worst batter on the team. To this day he recalls my encouragement more than the discouragement of setting the all-time Little League whiff record.

The Royal British Navy has a regulation which reads, "No officer shall speak discouragingly to another officer in the discharge of his duties." How we need to practice that regulation in our own homes!

TEACH THEM TO LOVE GOD

I close with this word to all of us parents about the use of our tongues. I am sure you want your kids to love God and live for Him, or you would not be reading this book. One of the greatest ways you can do that is to use your tongue to teach your children early, consistently, and continuously, the why and how of loving God. Another wise man named Moses gave this sage advice to parents a long time ago, but it is still priceless counsel today: "You shall love the LORD your God with all your heart, with all your soul, and with all your strength. And these words which I command you today shall be in your *heart*. You shall teach them diligently to your children, and shall *talk* of them when you sit in your house, when you walk by the way, when you lie down, and when you rise up" (Deut. 6:5–7).

God gave us our tongues specifically so that we might glorify Him. One of the best ways for us to do that is to teach our children to do likewise. A Sunday school teacher was asking her first-grade class the question, "Why do you love God?" One little boy gave this classic answer: "I guess it just runs in our family."

Dad, that kind of love can run in *your* family if, guided by a heart of wisdom, your tongue speaks God's truth to your children. Do it for their sake—and yours.

Chapter 4

LET ME TELL YOU
ABOUT THE BIRDS AND THE BEES

People talk all the time about oral contracep-
tion. The greatest form of oral contraception
I've ever come across is when I asked a girl to
go to bed with me and she said no!

—Woody Allen

T hough I do not condone Woody Allen's morals or cultural philosophy, his quote does illustrate that we need
to teach our kids not only to say no to premarital sex,
but also why no is the only answer. A cute story
affirms this parental necessity.

A third-grade boy named Johnny came in from school one day,
walked up to his daddy, and said, "Daddy, there's something I need
to ask you."

"What is it, son?"

"Daddy, where did I come from?"

The father nervously reached over and picked up some dia-
grams and pictures that he had been saving for this moment. He spent
the next forty-five minutes explaining the process of birth. With a
smug look on his face, inwardly congratulating himself on his great
job, he said, "Son, does that answer your question?"

"Not exactly," the boy replied.

"What do you mean, 'not exactly'?"

"Well, Billy, up the street, says he comes from Arkansas. I was just wondering where I came from."

When it comes to almost any subject our kids want to discuss, we dads can wing it without any problem—just name it. Sports? We can tell them how we just missed winning the Heisman Trophy—in high school! Cars? We can regale them with tales of the first car we ever owned that we bought with our own money—or built with our own hands! We can even discuss God without much of a problem; many dads wax eloquent in the role of "The Right Reverend Father."

There is one subject, however, that most dads never bring up. When their children do, "Mr. Macho" turns into "Mr. Nacho." The sure signs the subject has been broached are as follows (in no particular order): palpitations of the heart, sweaty palms, cotton mouth, dilation of the pupils, uncontrollable facial twitching—followed at some point by, "Go ask your mother," the only response the mouth can muster.

You guessed it. The subject is sex.

OUR TWO BIGGEST PROBLEMS

Many of us face a twofold problem concerning this sensitive but critically important topic. On the one hand, fathers are not talking or are waiting too late to talk, while children are not asking because they are getting their information somewhere else.

I think of the dad who quite nervously sat down with his fourth-grade son and said, "Son, don't you think it's time we had a talk about sex?" The little guy said, "Sure, Dad, what do you want to know?"

But there is still another problem: It has become obvious that education alone, especially school-based sex education, is not a panacea for all of our sexual problems. Compare the following two letters, the first a note written to Ann Landers. Read it and note Landers's response.

Dear Ann Landers:

I am heartbroken. My sixteen-year-old daughter has just been diagnosed with a very severe case of herpes.

I am beside myself. *"Melissa" has had plenty of sex education, and we have had many talks about safe sex and condoms.* When I asked her how this happened, she said she had no idea. Of course, Melissa would not tell me who she got it from. I did insist, however, that she inform the boy at once that he has a contagious disease. I pray she knows who he is, and that he was not one of several.

Please give me some advice as to how to deal with this nightmare. Melissa does not want to share this information with a therapist, and I don't dare tell my husband. He would hit the roof.

I am sick inside, not only for my daughter, but because of the ramifications of this affliction, which she will have for the rest of her life. I am also upset because there must have been something I *failed to get across to her.*

—Worried Sick in Pasadena

Dear Pasadena:

Cancel the guilt trip, mother. This is *not* your fault. Herpes is not a death sentence. Thousands of people who have it live normal lives. There are now highly effective drugs that can keep this infection well under control. [Now note carefully her next statement.]

Melissa needs to be educated.[1]

Did you note what Ann Landers said? "Melissa needs to be educated." Hello? If we learn anything from this letter, education was not the problem (in fact, a big part of the problem was the mother).

Now compare this with a letter written to the editor of the newspaper where I live. The note is honest and accurate, yet heartbreaking.

This is an open letter to your editors, Planned Parenthood, and all others endorsing school-based birth control clinics as the solution to teen pregnancies.

I'm an alumna of the sexual revolution, school Sex Education, and the contraceptive pill-pushing of the '60s and '70s. I had my first sex-ed class in 1965, and my first class of oral contraceptives in 1970 (at age 16 from Planned Parenthood, and without parental knowledge). I learned the dates, cycles, and methods forward and backward. Later I re-learned them in nursing school.

What did all of this enlightenment bring? Ask my first child who was killed via abortion. Ask my second one who was born illegitimately five years later (both were conceived *despite* my using contraceptives). Or, ask my subsequent children, who had to risk C-section births because I had contracted herpes during my years of educated sexual freedom. Ask me, I've had to struggle through mounds of sorrow and guilt because of my mistakes.

Is my story rare? Hardly. Although we taught school sex-ed for more than a decade, teen pregnancies have sky-rocketed to epidemic numbers, and despite readily available confidential contraceptives, abortions soar at 1.5 million per year in America.

I also haven't heard what your solution would be for sexually transmitted diseases, which are *already* of epidemic proportions. These diseases often cause permanent sterility, cervical cancer (via virus called HPV—or genital warts), neonatal illnesses, and now even death via AIDS.

Are you prepared to handle even higher numbers of sexually transmitted diseases and their tragic consequences in our teen population? When will you admit that sex education, when taught in a moral vacuum, has been a miserable failure? Instead, you want to throw more of the same at us.

Will scores of teens have to die from AIDS before our moral teachings finally change?

My solution? While our schools and churches are teaching kids to "just say no" to drugs, endorse the same philosophy about pre-marital and promiscuous sex. Insist that movies and TV also clean up their acts by boycotting the offensive ones. Make the cool and smart thing be to wait! It would protect their health and very lives, sharply decrease pregnancies and abortions, save millions of dollars, and curb disease.

I'd give anything to have wised up earlier because my education brought nothing but lifelong bitter lessons which can never be undone.[2]

Believing that God's law was written in pencil, we are living in a culture that passes out erasers. Sex Education is primarily a "con" job pushing nothing except *con*traceptives and *con*doms—but it's not working. Since 1970, the federal government has spent $3 billion to promote contraception and "safe sex." In the twenty years since the inception of federal family-planning programs, there has been an 87 percent rise in pregnancies for teenagers between the ages of fifteen through nineteen.[3] Unplanned births have risen 61 percent,[4] and syphilis rates have risen 60 percent for teenagers fifteen through nineteen since 1985.[5]

Everybody is talking about birth control, but nobody is talking about *self-control*. If you put Planned Parenthood in charge of traffic safety, I have an idea they would teach our children how to dodge cars instead of teaching them to stay off the freeway!

How would you feel if your children were taught they could shoot a gun at anybody they wanted to, as long as that person was wearing a bullet-proof vest? That is exactly what our kids are being taught when it comes to sex. What they are not being taught is that often somebody forgets to wear their vest, or in some cases the vest is defective.

HOME: THE RIGHT PLACE FOR SEX EDUCATION

The sad fact is, our children are getting their sex education in schools, the theater, the television, magazines, billboards, and computers—but not at home. Solomon wisely observed about the person who goes wrong in the area of sex. "He shall die for lack of instruction, and in the greatness of his folly he shall go astray" (Prov. 5:23). Did you notice how he lamented the lack of proper sex education? Today, our children are dying physically from venereal disease, emotionally from guilt, and spiritually from sexual sin—and all because of the lack of proper instruction.

For too long, both pastors and fathers have kept their heads in the sand, hoping this topic would just go away. But the subject cannot be avoided. George Gallup, the famous pollster, has stated, "There's no question about it, the sex-related issues are going to be the most important issues facing all churches in the foreseeable future. Abortion, AIDS, pre-marital sex, homosexuality—all those are going to be at the vortex."[6]

I am going to make a statement that may startle you at first, so stay with me. I believe that sex education *is* the answer—as long as it involves the right teacher, the right classroom, and the right curriculum. The right teacher is you, Dad; the right classroom is your home; and the right curriculum is the Bible.

Fellow dads, our children need fathers who will stand tall, be firm, and shoot straight about sex. Studies show that *parental involvement is the single most critical factor affecting the sexual activity of teens.* A study of ten thousand high school sophomores, conducted by the U.S. Department of Education, found that *strong parental values and parental supervision* have the most significant effect on teens' sexual activity. Parents who had a close relationship with their teenage daughter and supervised her school work and activities were able by 42 percent to curb the likelihood that their daughter would become pregnant.[7]

Solomon got involved early and strongly in the lives of his own kids in educating them about God's perspective on sex. The three largest sections in Proverbs dealing with one topic are found in chapters 5 through 7. In chapters 5 and 6 Solomon dealt extensively with premarital sex—fornication. He devoted almost the entirety of chapter 7 to extramarital sex—adultery. In between, he gave a frank discussion of sex within the will of God.

DANGER AHEAD!

Though his treatment of sex may sound negative at first, you will find Solomon was not saying that sex is dirty, but that it can be dangerous. In chapter 7, drawing from both divine wisdom and human experience, he vividly detailed three steps to sexual catastrophe. You find there a young man who was susceptible, an immoral woman who was available, and illicit sex that was desirable. When that combination appears, bad things are not only possible, but probable. Let's look at the three steps to sexual catastrophe.

STEP #1: SEXUAL SIN BEGINS WITH FOOLISH EXPOSURE

> For at the window of my house
> I looked through my lattice,
> And saw among the simple,
> I perceived among the youths,
> A young man devoid of understanding,
> Pssing along the street near her corner;
> And he took the path to her house. (Prov. 7:6–8)

Right away, we see mistake number one this young man makes, which is being in the wrong place, at the wrong time, with the wrong person.

We can turn that around and provide a positive lesson for our kids: *You cannot make a wrong move if you're not in the wrong place, with the wrong person, at the wrong time.* The first lesson to teach our children about sex is this: If you don't want to get burned, stay out of the kitchen.

You cannot get hooked on cocaine if you never use it. You cannot become an alcoholic if you never drink it. You cannot commit sexual sin if you do not allow yourself to get into the wrong situation.

Of course, it is impossible to escape completely from situations and people who may be potentially dangerous. But as Martin Luther wisely said, "I can't stop birds from flying over my head, but I can stop them from building a nest in my hair."

I heard about one elderly gentleman who noticed a little boy going around and around the block on his tricycle. This went on for about two hours. Finally the old man stopped the boy and said, "Son, aren't you getting tired? You've been going around this block all morning."

"I'm running away from home," replied the little boy.

"But you're not running away from home. You're just going around the block," objected the old man.

"No, I am running away from home," insisted the boy, "but my mommy said I couldn't cross the street."

The fact is, we are all prone to wander; but God has laid down the law and said there are certain boundaries we must not cross, certain places we should never go, and certain people we should never accompany. There is never a right time to be in the wrong place with the wrong person.

Incidentally, what a lot of parents call trust, I call neglect. Psychologist Henry Brandt tells how his son got upset with him when Brandt would not permit him to go out alone in a car with a girl down to the lake after dark. "What's wrong, Dad?" demanded the son. "Don't you trust me?"

"In a car, alone at night, in front of a lake, with a beautiful girl?" Brandt asked. "I wouldn't trust me. Why should I trust you?"[8]

STEP #2: SEXUAL SIN CONTINUES WITH FLIRTATIOUS EXCITEMENT

> So she caught him and kissed him;
> With an impudent face she said to him:
> "I have peace offerings with me;
> Today I have paid my vows.
> So I came out to meet you,
> Diligently to seek your face,
> And I have found you.
> I have spread my bed with tapestry,
> Colored coverings of Egyptian linen.
> I have perfumed my bed
> With myrrh, aloes, and cinnamon.
> Come, let us take our fill of love
>   until morning;
> Let us delight ourselves with love."
>   (Prov. 7:13–18)

This picture is three thousand years old, but it can quickly be brought up to date. The bed could be a waterbed or the back seat of a car. The linens could be thick carpet in front of a fireplace. The spices could be beer, pizza, and soft music playing in the background.

Notice how she used his eyes and his ears as a pipeline to his heart. Flattery was the bait and her tongue was the hook. Solomon often referred to the sexual dangers of flattery:

> To deliver you from the immoral woman,
> From the seductress who
>   flatters with her words. (Prov. 2:16)

> For the lips of an immoral
>   woman drip honey,
> And her mouth is smoother
>   than oil. (Prov. 5:3)

To keep you from the evil woman,
From the flattering tongue of a
    seductress. (Prov. 6:24)

That they may keep you from
    the immoral woman,
From the seductress who
    flatters with her words. (Prov. 7:5)

With her enticing speech she
    caused him to yield,
With her flattering lips she
    seduced him. (Prov. 7:21)

Sweet talk can lead to a sour experience which can poison a life. Flattery is God's "alarm clock" saying, "Let the buyer beware."

STEP #3: SEXUAL SIN ALWAYS LEADS TO A FATAL EXPERIENCE

Listen to the way Eugene Peterson, in his groundbreaking translation, *The Message*, translates two passages in this section on sex:

> Soon she has him eating out of her hand, bewitched by her honeyed speech. Before you know it, he is trotting behind her, like a calf led to the butcher shop, like a stag lured into ambush and then shot with an arrow, like a bird flying into a net, not knowing that its flying life is over. (7:21–23)

> The lips of a seductive woman are oh so sweet, her soft words are oh so smooth. But it won't be long before she's gravel in your mouth, a pain in your gut, a wound in your heart. She's dancing down the primrose path to death; she's headed straight for hell and taking you with her. (5:3–5)[9]

Whether you are a bum, a senator, an athlete, or a minister, there is a payday someday for sexual sin. People talk, husbands hear, pregnancies occur, diseases spread, and guilt festers. The week I was writing this chapter, Dick Morris—a chief advisor to the president of the United States, accustomed to walking the hallways of highest power—resigned because of an illicit affair with a $200-an-hour prostitute.

Let me give you three pieces of advice—no, make that three commands—to give to your sons and daughters every time they go out on a date:

Rule #1: Keep every button buttoned.

Rule #2: Keep every zipper zipped.

Rule #3: Keep every piece of clothing on.

This is frank talk, but it is the kind of talk our kids need when they enter the dating world of today.

THE FIRE THAT BURNS

Solomon made it plain to his kids that they might have champagne today, but real pain would come tomorrow. Using the canvas of Scripture, Solomon painted one of the most powerful pictures of the destructive power of sexual promiscuity to be found anywhere. Again, listen to Peterson's rendition:

> Can you build a fire in your lap and not burn your pants? Can you walk barefoot on hot coals and not get blisters? It's the same when you have sex with your neighbor's wife: touch her and you'll pay for it, no excuses. (Prov. 6:27–29)

There are two big lies our children are being told today about sex, and Solomon took care of both of them. The first lie is: Nobody suffers the consequences. Yet Solomon tells us sexual sin always leaves several types of scars.

THE SCAR OF EMOTIONAL DISTRESS

I find it interesting that Solomon compares sexual sin to being burned with fire. Doctors tell us that burns cause the most horrible scars the human body can suffer. They are the most obvious, the most painful, and the most resistant to corrective surgery. Nobody knows the anguish and guilt teenagers are under today because of the sexual revolution. Let me give you this one statistic: *Nonvirgins are six times as likely to commit suicide as virgins.*[10]

THE SCAR OF PHYSICAL DISEASE

Solomon said in Proverbs 5:11, "You mourn at last, when your flesh and your body are consumed." You should not be surprised to learn the following:

- One out of every five Americans are now infected with a viral sexually-transmitted disease (STD)—that's fifty-six million people.

- There are twelve million new sexually transmitted infections every year—two-thirds to people under twenty-six and one-fourth to teenagers.[11]

- Thirty-three thousand people a day contract a venereal disease, including six thousand teenagers.

- Twenty years ago there were four types of STDs among teenagers; today there are more than thirty.

- At the present rate, one in four Americans, between the ages of fifteen and fifty-five, eventually will acquire an STD.[12]

Rather than say anything else, I will let a medical doctor speak:

> The sexual revolution is over, said Dennis Maki, director of University of Wisconsin's Infectious Disease Department.
> In a *New York Daily News* article, Dr. Maki said, "Having promiscuous sex is close to 'suicidal behavior' because of the risk of exposure to

AIDS—a sexually-transmitted disease that kills 90 percent of its victims within five years of diagnosis.
. . .

In a powerful editorial supporting sexual fidelity, the *Journal of the American Medical Association* called for an end to sexual permissiveness to stop the spread of AIDS.

The *Journal* (the largest-circulating journal in the world) criticized the sexual mores of our time:

> It was the age of over-indulgence . . . of tolerance for anything and anybody . . . of anti-celibacy. . . . it was the age when homosexuality came out of the closet. . . . it was the age of easy irresponsible oversex, abortion-on-demand, chlamydia, and genital herpes, and it was the age of AIDS.

The editors concluded: This is a great time to practice sexual monogamy.[13]

THE SCAR OF MORAL DISGRACE

The adulterous person will wind up saying, "I was on the verge of total ruin, in the midst of the assembly and congregation" (Prov. 5:14). Fornication and adultery are "natural born killers." They not only kill the body; they kill reputations, testimonies, spiritual vitality, clear consciences, marriages, and peace with God.

THE SCAR OF SPIRITUAL DEFEAT

God can forgive sexual sin, but study the life of King David and you will find that he was never restored to his former power or position. The tree of promiscuity always bears bitter fruit. Though the wound heals, the scar always remains.

May I just stop right here and say a word to all of us dads? I'd like to quote for you a brief book excerpt that I have placed in the flyleaf of my Bible. I think you'll see why I put it there:

Following is the incomplete list of what you have in store after your immorality is found out.

- Your mate will experience the anguish of betrayal, shame, rejection, heartache, and loneliness. No amount of repentance will soften those blows.

- Your mate can never again say that you are a model of fidelity. Suspicion will rob her or him of trust.

- Your escapade(s) will introduce to your life and your mate's life the very real probability of a sexually transmitted disease.

- The total devastation your sinful actions will bring to your children is immeasurable. Their growth, innocence, trust, and healthy outlook on life will be severely and permanently damaged.

- The heartache you will cause your parents, your families, and your peers is indescribable.

- The embarrassment of facing other Christians who once appreciated you, respected you, and trusted you will be overwhelming.

- If you were engaged in the Lord's work, you will suffer the immediate loss of your job and the support of those with whom you worked. The dark shadow will accompany you everywhere and forever. Forgiveness won't erase it.

- Your fall will give others license to do the same.

- The inner peace you enjoyed will be gone.

- You will never be able to erase the fall from your (or others') mind. This will remain indelibly etched on your life's record regardless of your later return to your senses.

- The name of Jesus Christ, whom you once honored, will be tarnished, giving the enemies of faith further reason to sneer and jeer.[14]

Dad, the price of sexual sin is too high and the cost is too great. It is a bad bargain to trade the birthright of a clear conscience for the pottage of temporary sexual satisfaction.

SEX IS BEST WHEN SEX IS RIGHT

The second deadly lie that needs to be destroyed is that "Everybody is doing it." A September 1990 study from the Public Health Service of the Department of Health and Human Services shows that nearly 65 percent of all American females under the age of eighteen are still virgins. Even in the ages fifteen to nineteen, nearly 50 percent of the girls have *never* had sex.[15]

Remember that Solomon said sex is like a fire. That means it can be either powerfully constructive or powerfully destructive. Fire can heat your house when it is controlled, or burn it to the ground if it is uncontrolled. On the other hand, the best thing to put on a fire to keep it under control is water.

That is exactly what Solomon suggested:

> Drink water from your own cistern,
> And running water from your own well.
> Should your fountains be dispersed abroad,
> Streams of water in the streets?
> Let them be only your own,
> And not for strangers with you.
> Let your fountain be blessed,
> And rejoice with the wife of your youth.
> As a loving deer and a graceful doe,
> Let her breasts satisfy you at all times;
> And always be enraptured with her love.
> (Prov. 5:15–19)

Do you see how Solomon spoke of marital sex? He used the metaphors of water, cistern, well, fountain, and streams. When you understand his culture, you see why these images came to his mind.

In the ancient Near East, to have your own spring, well, or cistern was considered as valuable as gold. Clean water was a precious commodity. What Solomon was saying to his children is this: Why drink from the polluted water that comes from the sewer of promiscuous sex when, if you wait, you can drink the clean water that comes from the well of a devoted spouse?

Solomon was millennia ahead of his time, for he was impressing two truths on his children's hearts:

1. True love waits.

2. True love is worth the wait.

No one in history has ever regretted being a virgin on their wedding night. There is one thing we all have when we are born, and that is purity. Our children need to learn that when they marry they don't *lose* their purity, they *share* their purity. Purity shared in marriage lasts forever, but purity wasted before marriage is lost forever.

There is nothing as beautiful as sex with the right person, at the right place, at the right time, in the will of God. A story I heard years ago says it best, and I wish every parent would tell it to their sons and daughters, particularly as they begin to enter the years of courtship and marriage.

A girl living fast and loose was trying to entice one of her friends, who was pure, to join her in a jet-set lifestyle. The pure girl said to the loose girl, "I want to tell you something. Any time I want to become like you are, I can. But you can never again become like I am."

Let's teach our children and our teenagers that their bodies belong first to God. If they will give their bodies first to Him and then later to the spouse He gives to them, then they will enjoy God's beautiful gift of sex the way He has planned it from the beginning.

Chapter 5

HOW TO LOWER
YOUR TEMPER (-ATURE)

When anger enters the mind, wisdom departs.

—Thomas á Kempis

Guess what the following sentences describe: "Respiration deepens; the heart beats more rapidly; the arterial pressure rises; the blood is shifted from the stomach and intestines to the heart, central nervous system, and the muscles; the processes of the alimentary canal cease; sugar is freed from the reserves in the liver; the spleen contracts and discharges its contents of concentrated corpuscles, and adrenaline is secreted."[1]

What was your guess? If you thought the paragraph described the physiological manifestation of anger, you chose correctly. Those are the words of Walter Cannon, a researcher at Harvard University.

Anybody can get angry—even the best of us. In an article titled "Only in America," *Fortune* magazine recorded a humorous, but tragic, story illustrating this very point:

> Honolulu—An anger-management counselor lost his temper and allegedly punched a man who arrived at a class drunk. The man lapsed into a coma and was declared brain dead.

Charles Mahuka . . . was arrested on suspicion of assaulting Miguel Conzales, 32 . . . at a church in Waianae.

Dora Hoopii-Spalding said Mahuka, 39, punched Conzales, knocked him to the ground, and hit him three more times. . . .

Conzales had been ordered to attend the anger-management class after he was arrested and accused of assaulting his girlfriend.

(As a footnote) Mahuka went to prison for stabbing a man with a fishing spear in 1986.[2]

Moses, David, the prophet Jonah, and Jesus all had one thing in common: They all got angry. Anger leaves tracks on the paths of life that are easy for anybody to find. One small spark of anger can start a raging fire that, in an instant, can consume a lifelong friendship.

There is a burning caldron of anger running over in our society, spilling into our schools, our government, and even our homes. More than 60 percent of the homicides in America are committed by angry family members.[3]

Most everyone knows that the number one killer in America is heart disease. But would it interest you to know further that the number one cause of heart disease is—you guessed it—anger? Dr. Redford Williams, director of Duke University's Behavioral Medicine Research Center, stated, "The hostility and anger associated with Type A behavior is the major contributor to heart disease in America."[4]

People who struggle with anger are five times as likely to suffer coronary heart disease as the average person. People with heart disease more than double their risk of a heart attack when they get angry.[5] Of course, there is a difference between anger and mere aggravation.

A little girl was doing her homework and asked her father to explain the difference between anger and aggravation. He went to the telephone, dialed a number, and had his daughter listen in on the conversation. When the other person answered, her dad said, "Hello, is Melvin there?"

"There's no one here named Melvin," came the reply. "Why don't you look up numbers before you dial them?"

The father waited a moment and then dialed the number again. He said, "Hello, is Melvin there?"

The man yelled, "Now look! I just told you that there is no Melvin here! Don't call this number again!" Then he slammed down the receiver.

The father looked at the daughter and said, "Honey, that was anger. Now let me show you aggravation."

He dialed the number again, and a voice roared out, *"Hello!"* The man calmly said, "This is Melvin; have there been any calls for me?"

ONE LETTER SHORT OF DANGER

One of the most important lessons fathers can teach their children (and you had better teach them early and often) is how to control their tempers. *Anger* is only one letter short of *danger,* and it behooves all of us, in our violent hair-trigger society, to learn how to manage our anger.

If you dads would like to do a little exercise that will both send you soaring and sinking at the same time, ask your kids these two questions:

"What is my greatest strength as a father?"

"What is my greatest weakness as a father?"

I took the plunge and asked my two oldest sons these questions (separately), and I got identical responses from both. They agree that my greatest strength is, "You have taught me about God—how to love Him and live for Him." I must admit the old head did swell for just a moment.

But only for a moment. Their answer to the second question saw to that. What was my biggest weakness? They both replied with lightning speed, "Your temper—you just don't have very much patience." If there are any dads out there who, like me, suffer a similar problem (and perhaps are seeing that problem reproduced in your kids' lives), let's take this medicine together!

WHEN THE THERMOSTAT
SHOULD BE TURNED UP

I want to let you in on two well-kept secrets about anger. Secret number one is this: Anger is an emotion God Himself experiences.

Did you know it is not always a sin to be angry? If it were, then Jesus was a sinner because Jesus became angry. Yet we know that Jesus was without sin (even though He was not without anger). In fact, all three persons in the Godhead get angry. God the Father knows what it is to be angry. No less than eighteen times the Old Testament speaks of "the anger of the Lord." To those who want to emphasize the love of God exclusively against the holiness of God, Psalm 7:11 is a show-stopping verse: "God is a just judge, and God is angry with the wicked every day."

The word *angry* in Hebrew literally means "to foam at the mouth." Do you know how angry you have to be to foam at the mouth? Yet God is that angry with the wicked. To be sure, He loves the sinner, but He absolutely despises the sin.

God the Son also knows what it is to be angry. On one occasion a man with a withered hand came to Jesus to be healed on the Sabbath Day. The hypocritical Pharisees were watching to see if Jesus would perform what they thought was an ungodly act. We read in Mark 3:5, "He [Jesus] had looked around at them with anger."

Even God the Holy Spirit can be angry. First Samuel 11:6 tells us, "Then the Spirit of God came upon Saul when he heard this news, and his anger was greatly aroused." It was the Spirit's presence in Saul that drove him to anger.

Aristotle once said, "Anybody can become angry; that is easy. But to be angry with the right person, and to the right degree, and at the right time, and for the right purpose, and in the right way; that is not within everybody's power, and that is not easy." He was right. It is not easy, but it is possible. It is possible to be "good and angry" at the same time.

But consider secret number two: Anger is a God-given emotion. Solomon's father, David, said, "Be angry, and do not sin" (Ps. 4:4). A person who always gets angry is a fool, but a person who never gets angry is a wimp. A well-known preacher of yesteryear, Henry Ward Beecher, made a strong statement about anger that we who live in a crumbling society need to hear again: "A man that does not know how to be angry does not know how to be good. A man that does not know how to be shaken to his heart's core with indignation over things evil is either a fungus or a wicked man."[6]

There are at least two occasions when we ought to be angry. The first is when *God's people openly disobey Him.* I'm sure Solomon remembered a time when God got angry with him. The Bible records this incident in 1 Kings 11:9: "So the LORD became angry with Solomon, because his heart had turned from the LORD God of Israel, who had appeared to him twice."

Dads, there is a lesson we can learn here from God the Father. When your children willfully, openly, defiantly rebel against you and your God-given authority, you *ought* to be angry, and you *ought* to channel that anger into constructive correction of your children. Part of your job in rearing your children is to teach your children how to control their anger, not how to eliminate it altogether.

One of the greatest ways to do this is to use the anger of Jesus as an example. As we have said, even Jesus got angry, as the following account confirms: "Now the Passover of the Jews was at hand, and Jesus went up to Jerusalem. And He found in the temple those who sold oxen and sheep and doves, and the money changers doing business. When He had made a whip of cords, He drove them all out of the temple, with the sheep and the oxen, and poured out the changers' money and overturned the tables. And He said to those who sold doves, 'Take these things away! Do not make My Father's house a house of merchandise!'" (John 2:13–16).

Can you see Jesus cracking that whip, singeing the backsides of those money-mongers? Can you see patches of wool still floating in the air that had been lashed off those sheep? I'd bet that even ten minutes later you could still hear His voice, echoing off the temple walls! To see those religious hypocrites tripping over their tunics and falling over each other while setting the Guinness World Book of Records for getting out of church must have been a hoot! As Tom Cruise said in the film *Mission Impossible,* when asked if he was upset: "You've never seen me *upset.*"

Well, Jesus was more than a little upset—he was *angry.* But as I taught my kids just recently, He was angry at the *right place* (the temple—though anger at individuals should be privately expressed most of the time); at the *right people* (no problem with mistaken identity); for the *right reason* (over a wrong done to others—in this case, God—not Himself); at the *right time* (the issue was dealt with immediately; though, at times, anger may be better expressed at another time so as to avoid humiliating someone); in the *right way* (in this case, a raised voice and a whip was necessary; at other times, neither will be).

Dad, early on when your child gets angry, use these five criteria to help your kids determine if their anger was appropriate under the circumstances. Teach them to express their anger only as a last resort, never in retaliation; and above all, remind them that Jesus got angry only when others were being wronged, not Himself.

There is at least one other occasion when we ought to be angry, and that is when *people in authority and power stand against what is right for what is wrong, and they hurt others in the process.* Listen to this scathing passage of Scripture that sounds like it could have been written in the twentieth century:

> Woe to those who call evil good,
>   and good evil;
> Who put darkness for light, and
>   light for darkness;
> Who put bitter for sweet, and
>   sweet for bitter!
> Woe to those who are wise in
>   their own eyes,
> And prudent in their own sight!
> Woe to men mighty at drinking wine,
> Woe to men valiant for mixing
>   intoxicating drink,
> Who justify the wicked for a bribe,

And take away justice from the
    righteous man!
Therefore, as the fire devours the stubble,
And the flame consumes the chaff,
So their root will be as rottenness,
And their blossom will ascend like dust;
Because they have rejected the
    law of the LORD of hosts,
And despised the word of the
    Holy One of Israel.
Therefore the anger of the
    LORD is aroused against His people;
He has stretched out His hand against them
And stricken them,
And the hills trembled.
Their carcasses were as refuse
    in the midst of the streets.
For all this His anger is not turned away,
But His hand is stretched out still.
    (Isa. 5:20–25)

It is not wrong to be angry at wrong, particularly when that wrong is being done to someone else. *We ought to be angry:*

- Over the deaths of millions of innocent, unborn babies whose lives are snuffed out each year by abortion

- Over a sex-crazed, profanity-filled movie industry that is polluting the minds of young and old alike

- Over cowardly politicians who do what is politically expedient instead of what is morally right

- Over a liquor industry that is killing more people, wrecking more homes, and ruining more lives than anything else in America

- Over prejudice and injustice done unto others just because of the color of their skin

75

Use this rule of thumb to help you gauge when anger is right and when it is wrong. *The way to be angry, and not sin, is to be angry at nothing but sin.* The old Puritan, Thomas Watson, put it best when he said, "That anger is without sin that is against sin."[7]

I remember hearing a preacher by the name of Jack Hyles tell how his child once had been assigned to read a book filled with foul language and questionable "situations." The more Dr. Hyles perused the book, the angrier he got.

Eventually he marched up to the principal's office, went in, and politely but firmly said, "My son is *not* going to read this book, he *will* be assigned a different book fit to read, and he will *not* be marked down because of it."

The principal, taken aback and intending to argue with Dr. Hyles, said , "But—"

Dr. Hyles interrupted and said softly but sternly, "No ifs, ands, or buts about it. He *will not* be forced to read this book, and he *will* be assigned another one. Is that clear?"

The principal replied, "All right, Dr. Hyles, but I don't understand the fuss. After all, the language in that book is no worse than what is written on the bathroom walls."

Dr. Hyles just smiled and said, "Yes, and when that becomes required reading, I'll be back!"

It is difficult, to be sure, but not impossible to be angry at wrong but not be wrong in being angry. Indeed, many of the problems in our culture today stem from a lack of, shall we say, righteous indignation.

WHEN THE FURNACE IS TO BE TURNED OFF

Most every verse in Proverbs casts anger in a negative light because, most of the time, our anger is an expression of sin. Let's be honest. Occasionally, we may become angry for a good reason; however, well over 90 percent of the time (and that is a conservative estimate) we become angry because we are selfish, impatient, irritated, or hurt over the way we have been treated.

As you notice the occasions when Jesus got angry (which were few), something jumps out immediately: Jesus *never* got angry over what someone did to *Him*. Jesus never retaliated or lashed out at anyone who wronged Him. Even when His executioners nailed Him to the cross, He said, "Father, forgive them, for they know not what they do." Jesus grew angry when *others* were hurt or wronged.

So often our problem is just the opposite. I heard about two boys who walked into the dentist's office. One boy said, "Doc, we've got a lot of things we want to do today. We want to go outside and play; we don't want to spend all day in the dentist's office. I've got a tooth that's got to come out, and I want it to come out right now. Forget the Novocain and the gas, just get your pliers and pull it out."

"Well, son, I certainly do admire your courage," the dentist replied. "Which tooth is it?"

The boy turned to his buddy and said, "Show him your tooth, Tommy."

Why is it that the pain we cause others affects us so little? Isn't it true that we too often get angry at things we shouldn't get angry over, while we don't get angry over things that should anger us?

I have learned that the more self-centered we are, the more quick-tempered we will be. It is that quick temper, that volcanic eruption which occurs when someone invades our territory, that is so dangerous.

THE COST OF ANGER

I remember vividly my first trip to Israel. We flew into Amman, Jordan, and the next morning we visited Mount Nebo. As I stood on that plateau looking across the Jordan River to the fertile Jordan valley with its lush vegetation, verdant vineyards, and groves of banana trees, my mind went back to one of the greatest Jewish leaders ever—Moses.

Moses was a great leader, a meek man for the most part; but on one occasion, his anger got the best of him and caused him to disobey God. Because of his outburst, God prohibited Moses from entering the promised land. The closest he got was seeing it from Mount Nebo before he died.

Moses stood on that very same site, looking at a land flowing with milk and honey. I can hardly imagine how his heart ached to cross that Jordan River with his people and plant his feet on the sacred soil God had promised to Israel. He was oh-so close—yet so far away—and the invisible barrier that kept him out was his anger. One fitful moment cost Moses the opportunity he had spent his life waiting for.

Nothing can cook your goose quicker than boiling anger. It is an incontrovertible truth that when a person's temper gets the best of him, it reveals the worst of him. It was the humorist, Will Rogers, who said, "People who fly into a rage seldom make a good landing."

Wise old Benjamin Franklin once wrote in *Poor Richard's Almanac*, "Take this remark from Richard, poor and lame, whate'er's begun in anger ends, in shame." If you are prone to lose your temper quickly or often (actually, people don't lose their temper; they find it), consider carefully what Solomon said about a quick-tempered person.

First, a quick temper is *stupid*. "A quick-tempered man acts foolishly, and a man of wicked intentions is hated" (Prov. 14:17). If you are a person with a hair-trigger temper, you are a fool (incidentally, if that makes you angry, you just proved it).

Solomon also said a quick temper is *divisive*. "A wrathful man stirs up strife" (Prov. 15:18a). You show me someone who has a quick temper, who flies off the handle at the least little thing, and I'll show you a person who is argumentative, contrary, always fighting or fussing with someone—and has very few friends.

But even that's not the worst of it. According to Solomon, a quick temper is also *destructive*. "A man of great wrath will suffer punishment; for if you rescue him, you will have to do it again" (Prov. 19:19). If you consistently, constantly, and continuously lose your temper, ultimately you will be the one who loses. You will lose friends, you will lose the love of your wife, and you will lose the respect of your colleagues and your children. It may even cause you to lose your health.

John Hunter, a physiologist who had a severe heart condition, said, "My life is at the mercy of the person who can make me angry. . . . The first scoundrel that gets me angry will kill me."

People are in jail, on death row, or even dead today, because of one thing: anger.

KEEP THE FIRE BURNING
BUT THE LID ON THE POT

I want to make as dogmatic a statement as I can: If you are a Christian, you *can* and *should* control your temper. Don't blame your anger on someone or something else. Solomon made this astute observation: "He who is slow to anger is better than the mighty, and he who rules his spirit than he who takes a city" (Prov. 16:32).

You *can* be slow to anger, and you *can* control your spirit. Indeed, as a Christian, you have the Holy Spirit within you, and part of the fruit of the Spirit is "self control" (Gal 5:23).

Anger is like a river. A river controlled can generate enough electricity to power an entire city. But if allowed to overflow its banks, it can become a raging flood that destroys everything in its path. As surely as a river can be controlled, so can your temper.

You can control your temper if you really want to, and I will prove it to you. Have you ever been in a bitter argument in your home, either with your wife or one of your kids? I'm talking about the old-fashioned kind when everybody is yelling at the top of their lungs, going at it tooth and tong. About that time the phone rings, and instantly you pick it up and answer in a soft, controlled tone, "Hello-o-o-o. May I help you?" What happened? You just proved that your anger can be controlled and tamed.

Wise old Solomon gave some wise old advice on how to handle an age-old problem. Dad, these are life lessons you can use and pass on to your kids.

THINK FAST, TALK LATER

"He who is slow to wrath has great understanding, but he who is impulsive exalts folly" (Prov. 14:29). Not everything is worth getting angry about. The more calmly you see a situation, the more clearly you will see how to handle it. If you have a quick temper, follow some good advice I heard recently: "When you are angry, count to ten before you speak. If you are real angry, count to a hundred—and then don't say anything."

KEEP YOUR HAND ON THE THROTTLE

"A fool gives full vent to his anger, but a wise man keeps himself under control" (Prov. 29:11, NIV). Anger is to be a servant, not a master. Either you control your temper, or your temper controls you. Don't allow your temper to put you on a leash; you keep it on a leash.

Teach your kids to ask two questions when they feel their temperature rising: (1) Is this really worth my anger? If the answer is yes, then (2) is this the best way, place, and time to express my anger? I know it is hard to do this in the heat of the moment, but emotions can be tamed and the temper can be trained.

When I first started driving, if someone pulled in front of me, they got an ear full of horn. Today, I let it slide. Why? First, I have matured and mellowed somewhat; but the fact that someone might either shoot me or run me off the road has also had something to do with it. In these days, controlling our tempers may save our lives!

LOOK UP AND OVER

"The discretion of a man makes him slow to anger, and his glory is to overlook a transgression" (Prov. 19:11). Never kill a fly with a sledgehammer. When you are wronged, the question is not, are you big enough to do something about it? The question is, are you big enough not to?

I heard about two brothers who got into an awful fight. The mother ran upstairs to break it up, and when she asked how the fight got started the older brother said, "It all started when he hit me back!"

We, as well as our kids, need to learn that in God's eyes it is glory if we are big enough not to hit back. (Though I am not advocating pacifism in the case of a bully!)

WALK SLOW, RUN FAST

"A wrathful man stirs up strife, but he who is slow to anger allays contention" (Prov. 15:18). Solomon repeatedly admonished his children to "be slow to anger" (14:29; 15:18; 16:32; 19:11). If you are headed toward the house of anger, be slow to arrive and walk in, and extremely quick to run out the back door. Paul said, "Be angry, and do not sin: do not let the sun go down on your wrath" (Eph. 4:26).

Never store the acid of anger in the container of your body. Anger is an acid that can do more harm to the vessel in which it is stored than to anything on which it is poured. Like milk that sours, anger that is not quickly disposed of will curdle into the cancer of bitterness.

TALK SOFTLY AND CARRY AN OLIVE BRANCH

"A soft answer turns away wrath, but a harsh word stirs up anger" (Prov. 15:1). Have you ever noticed that a fire department almost never fights fire with fire? Water is almost always a better tool. In the same way, a soft reply to an angry comment is like putting the cold water of calmness on the fire of a hot temper.

The Speech Research Unit of Kenyon College has proved, through a series of tests, that when a person is shouted at, he almost universally shouts back. Researchers also discovered that it is possible to control another person's tone of voice by your own. If you keep your voice soft, not only will you avoid becoming angry, but you will most likely prevent the other person from becoming angry.

BE GOOD, OR BE GONE

"Make no friendship with an angry man, and with a furious man do not go, lest you learn his ways and set a snare for your soul" (Prov. 22:24–25). We become like the people we spend time with. If we spend time with angry and rebellious people, we will inevitably become angry and rebellious. (Dad, this is a strong reason why you need to be actively involved and in charge of the types of relationships your children establish.)

HOW ARE YOU GOING TO ACT?

A wonderful story illustrates perfectly the truth that we need to convey to our kids about anger. A certain man purchased a newspaper at a newsstand. He greeted the newsman very courteously, but in return he received very gruff and discourteous service; the vendor would rudely shove the newspaper in the man's face. The man, however, would politely smile and wish the newsman a nice day. This went on for several days until a friend asked, "Does he always treat you this rudely?"

"Unfortunately, he does."

"And are you always so polite and friendly to him?"

"Yes, I am."

"Why are you so nice to him when he is so rude to you?"

"Because I don't want *him* to decide how *I* am going to act."[8]

Dad, teach your kids that nobody can make them angry without their consent. We need to let God consecrate even the very emotion of anger, surrender it to His complete control, and use it for His glory. Under the power of the Holy Spirit, it can be done.

Chapter 6

TASTES GREAT, LESS FILLING—
SOUNDS GOOD, NOT TRUE

No man ever drank lard into his tub,
or flour into his sack,
nor meal into his barrel,
nor happiness into his home,
nor God into his heart.

—Benjamin Franklin

As I approach this chapter's topic, I am reminded of a Sunday school teacher who was trying to explain the dangers of alcohol to a class of little boys. She set a glass of clear water next to a glass of alcohol.

She dropped a few worms into the water, and they swam around. She then dropped a few worms into the alcohol, and they immediately curled up and died. Holding the glass of alcohol in one hand and the glass of water in the other, she said, "Now, boys, who can tell me the lesson this teaches us?"

One child raised his hand and said, "I know the lesson! If you ever get worms, drink a lot of alcohol."

Frankly, I know some readers will be like that child: concerning the topic of alcohol, they either *don't* get it or *won't* get it. When it comes to alcohol and drinking—whether socially, recreationally, or habitually—the attitude of many is, "Don't confuse me with the facts. My mind is made up." If you happen to be a drinker of any sort, would you "unmake your mind" long enough to give this chapter a fair hearing—if not for your sake, then at least for the possible well-being of your family?

ALCOHOL: THE ACCEPTED KILLER

Alcohol is a drug that claims more addicts than any other drug in America. Alcoholics outnumber drug addicts ten to one, and alcoholic deaths outnumber drug overdoses three to one. Alcohol causes more deaths than AIDS, heroin, cocaine, marijuana, and crack combined.[1]

There are those who protest the classification of alcohol as a drug, but Marvin Block, former chairman of the American Medical Association's Committee on Alcoholism, said, "Ours is a drug-oriented society, largely because of alcohol. Because of its social acceptance, alcohol is rarely thought of as a drug. But a drug it is, in scientific fact."[2]

Amazingly, it is the one drug that is accepted as legitimate by the vast majority of Americans. Therefore, it is available to young and old alike and is advertised profusely through television, radio, billboards, and at athletic stadiums throughout the country. We have been conditioned to believe that practically everybody drinks, and something is wrong with the persons who don't.

The average child will see alcohol consumed seventy-five thousand times on television before he reaches the legal drinking age. Every seven and one-half minutes on television, an alcoholic drink is offered to someone, and fifteen times out of sixteen the drink is accepted.[3] Seventy-six percent of people on television who are shown drinking anything at all will be drinking alcohol. Television actors will consume fourteen times more alcohol than soft drinks and fifteen times more alcohol than water. It seems as if every commercial during a televised athletic event reminds you that it "tastes great and is less filling."

I realize that to take on the topic of drinking, whether it is done in moderation or in excess, is to be a modern-day John the Baptist crying in the wilderness. Seventy-one percent of Americans drink, and the number of Americans who drink has doubled in the last twenty-five years. Seventy-five percent of all high school students drink, and by the twelfth grade 93 percent of the boys and 87 percent of the girls will have taken at least one drink.

Surprisingly, churchgoers may not be any more sympathetic to the message of this chapter than the general population. One-half of all ordained ministers drink, and one-third of all active churchgoers drink. Even in my own denomination, 48 percent of Southern Baptists drink, and an estimated 16 percent of those who do drink become alcoholics—a higher percentage than virtually any other religious group in the nation. Furthermore, one-fourth of all active Southern Baptist church teenagers have used alcohol in the past twelve months.[4]

It would have been easy for me to leave this chapter out of the book. After all, this is the day of ducking the issues rather than telling the truth. But since Solomon did not flinch in facing the topic of alcohol and drinking, neither will I. His basic philosophy was summed up in a simple, but strong statement:

> Wine is a mocker,
> Strong drink is a brawler,
> And whoever is led astray by
> it is not wise. (Prov. 20:1)

Though there is an encyclopedia of wisdom in that one verse, Solomon expanded on his thinking in the longest continuous passage on alcohol in the Bible, driving home his point with devastating force (see Prov. 23:29–35).

Dad, I am going to address this issue for the same reason Solomon did—*for the sake of our children.* Keep in mind as you read this chapter that alcohol use typically begins around the age of thirteen, but a full 35 percent of fourth graders (ages 9 through 10) have been pressured by classmates to drink.[5] Whatever you are going to teach your children about alcohol, you better teach them early, firmly, and consistently—because if you don't, their peers will. And you won't like the results.

THE WAKE OF "HURRICANE ALCOHOL"

Solomon didn't mince words when it came to the matter of drinking alcohol. He said,

> Wine is a mocker,
> Strong drink is a brawler,
> And whoever is led astray by
>   it is not wise. (Prov. 20:1)

Note the warning that the one who imbibes can be "led astray." The Hebrew word is *shah-gah*, meaning "to [cause to] go astray, stray, err." I find it very revealing that this term was used.

Solomon was not only saying that drunkenness leads one astray—that is a truism. He was making the observation that wine and strong drink have an inherent tendency to "lead one astray." But astray from what? *The path of wisdom!* As you will see shortly, moderation in drinking is often more of a problem than a solution to the question of alcohol.

Obviously, the overconsumption of alcohol makes a mockery (even a monkey!) out of one. Yet Solomon did not say, "Drunkenness is a mocker"; he said, "Wine is a mocker." As one commentary puts it, "The idea is that wine mocks the one who drinks it and beer makes him aggressive."[6]

Solomon dealt with drunkenness in several other passages. The clear implication here is that if one realizes what wine and strong drink are—a "mocker" and a "brawler"—and what they tend to do—"lead one astray"—the wise will avoid them altogether. In other words, as alcohol tends to lead one astray from the path of wisdom, so the path of wisdom will lead one away from alcohol!

Solomon's letter was filled with concern that his children not veer from the way of wisdom. It is interesting to note that in Proverbs Solomon specifically warned his children of three things that would cause them to leave the beaten path of success and "stray" into the swamp of failure.

We have already dealt with the first: the seductive, adulterous woman. Referring to the person who allows himself to be trapped by the adulterous woman, Solomon said, "In the greatness of his folly he shall *go astray*" (5:23b). Failure to use discretion in the area of sexual morality is a sure way to wander off into the wilderness of heartache and sorrow.

The second is the refusal to listen to the wise instruction of a godly father. "Cease listening to instruction, my son, and you will *stray* from the words of knowledge" (Prov. 19:27). Godly counsel from a spiritual parent is like a guardrail on the road of life, helping to keep your children from tumbling down the cliff of spiritual and moral defeat.

The third is drinking alcoholic beverages as described in Proverbs 20:1. In the end, alcohol turns what should be a highway of holiness and happiness into a rain-slickened, ice-covered road of disaster and even death. In the most articulate warning in the Bible concerning alcohol consumption, Proverbs 23:29–35, Solomon pointed to at least four types of bitter fruit that the root of alcoholic drink eventually bears:

1. Emotional problems: "woe" and "sorrow" (v. 29a)

2. Social problems: "contentions" and "complaints" (v. 29b)

3. Physical problems: "wounds" and "redness of eyes" (v. 29c)

4. Mental problems: "see strange things" and "utter perverse things" (v. 33)[7]

BUT DOES SOLOMON LIVE IN THE REAL WORLD?

The question is raised: Does experience in the real world bear out Solomon's reflection in his theological world? Well, dad, consider the following:

- The cost *financially* of "tastes great, less filling," is staggering. The use of alcohol and alcoholism cost the United States more than $98 billion in lost work time alone.[8]

- To combat the colossal crisis caused by the 15.3 million Americans who use or abuse alcohol, federal and state governments have enacted over one thousand laws since 1980.[9] (They say, "You can't legislate morality," but somebody sure is trying!)

- There are those who try to defend the licensing and selling of alcohol because of the tax revenue it generates. But what is left unsaid is that for every one dollar in revenue that alcohol brings, it costs eight dollars to clean up the mess that it leaves behind.[10]

- *Physically*, alcohol exacts a tremendous price as well. The consumption of alcohol has created the largest health problem in the United States when measured in terms of morbidity. It is the fourth largest cause of death after heart disease, cancer, and stroke.[11]

- Alcohol is responsible for 108,000 deaths a year, and sixty-two people are killed every day in an alcohol-related automobile accident.[12] (Valujet has one accident, and we shut them down cold. Yet the alcohol industry takes 62 lives *a day,* and we say nothing!) Alcohol reduces the life expectancy of a human being by an average of ten years.

- One-half of all homicides, one-third of all suicides, one-half of all fires, and one-half of all drownings, are directly due to alcohol. Furthermore, 50 percent of all traffic fatalities, 25 percent of all accidental deaths, 50 percent of all airplane crashes, 93 percent of all hit-and-run accidents, and 80 percent of all crime is directly due to the influence of alcohol.

- Worst of all, however, is the carnage alcohol leaves in its wake *domestically*. Separated or divorced men and women are more than three times as likely as married men and women to have been married to an alcoholic or a problem drinker (27.6% to 7.6%).[13]

- Recently, a survey within my own denomination showed that 85 percent of all children in our Baptist Children's Homes are there not because they are orphans, but because they had to leave homes that were broken by alcohol.

I doubt there is one father reading this book right now who cannot think of a marriage that has been destroyed, a wife who has been abused, or a child who has been emotionally devastated because of the scourge of alcohol.

There is no need to belabor the point. Your home may very well be the exception. Indeed, as far as we know from Scripture, Solomon never had any problem with alcohol. But he obviously had seen its great dangers and was warning his children—as we need to warn ours—that "tastes great" may be "less filling," but it is definitely "more killing!"

WHAT THE BIBLE *REALLY* SAYS ABOUT ALCOHOL

Contrary to popular opinion, there is little ambiguity in the Scriptures concerning alcohol and its consumption. Much confusion stems from equating alcoholic beverages described in the Bible with those bought, sold, and consumed today. Dad, the following discussion may be a tad technical, but I strongly encourage you to hang with me. The life you save by reading it may be that of your own child.

Notice that Solomon referred in Proverbs 20:1 to "wine" and "strong drink." These are beverages made from grapes and grains.[14] It is crucial for our study to consider the second term, "strong drink," first. The Hebrew term is *shay-kahr*. It refers to an intoxicating drink that would be made from barley, pomegranates, dates, apples, or honey.

It is important to note, however, that biblical scholars tell us that even this term "most likely [does] not [refer to] 'liquor' for there is no evidence of distilled liquor in ancient times."[15] Strong drink is universally condemned in the Bible. Priests were to avoid it (Lev. 10:8–9), as were kings (Prov. 31:4–5); Isaiah pronounced judgment on those who used it (Isa. 5:11). Norman L. Geisler, in an excellent article titled, "A Christian Perspective on Wine-drinking," says unequivocally: "God is opposed to using strong drink as a beverage."[16]

The other term, "wine," derives from the Hebrew *yah-yin*. This is the most common Old Testament word used for alcoholic drink, being found 141 times. It is a generic term. Sometimes it is used for an intoxicating drink and sometimes for a nonintoxicating drink.[17]

As do the rest of the Old Testament authors, Solomon made a distinction between wine and strong drink.[18] This is extremely important for several reasons. A New Testament scholar named Robert Stein researched the wine-drinking of the ancient world in both Jewish sources and the Bible. He made a fascinating discovery about the wine of Bible days, as compared to the wine of today.

The wine of biblical times was not like the wine that exists today. Stein's research uncovered the fact that wine in the days of Jesus, for example, was actually wine mixed with water. On average it would be three or four parts of water mixed with one part of wine. In other words, what the Bible calls wine was basically purified water.[19]

Stein points out that in the ancient world many beverages were unsafe to drink. Water could be made safe in one of several ways: it could be boiled, but this was tedious and costly. It could be filtered, but this was not always safe. The safest method was to put wine into the water to kill the germs (wine kills both germs and worms!), one part wine with three or four parts water.

So, as one Old Testament scholar and Hebrew expert put it: "Wine was the most intoxicating drink known in ancient times. All the wine was light wine, i.e., not fortified with extra alcohol. Concentrated alcohol was only known in the Middle Ages when the Arabs invented distillation . . . so what is now called liquor or strong drink (i.e., whiskey, gin, etc.) and the twenty percent fortified wines of today were unknown in Bible times."[20]

This sheds light on Solomon's admonition: "Do not look on the wine when it is red, when it sparkles in the cup" (Prov. 23:31). He was referring to wine unmixed with water. He was illustrating the poisonous bite and pernicious sting of undiluted wine ("At the last it bites like a serpent, and stings like a viper," v. 32).

Today's wine has a much higher alcohol content than wine in Bible days. In fact, Dr. Stein noted that in New Testament times, one would have to drink twenty-two glasses of wine in order to consume the alcohol in only two martinis today.[21]

In summary, though fermented wine was drunk in Bible times and though the Bible approves of wine-drinking, one needs to remember that the alcoholic content of ancient wine was much less than that of wine today. What is consumed today is *not* the wine of the New Testament! To equate the two would be like comparing apples and oranges. So, Dr. Geisler concluded: "Therefore, Christians ought not drink wine, beer, or other alcoholic beverages, for they are actually 'strong drink' and are forbidden in Scripture. Even ancient pagans did not drink what some Christians drink today!"[22]

LEGITIMATE USES OF ALCOHOL

Let me hasten to add that legitimate uses of wine and alcohol are found in the Bible. Sometimes it was used as a medicine. Evidently Timothy had stomach problems, and Paul told him "use a little wine for your stomach's sake and your frequent infirmities" (1 Tim. 5:23). Wine, in the ancient world, was oftentimes used as a laxative. Paul prescribed diluted wine as medicine for Timothy's digestive problems.

Sometimes wine was used as a sedative or a pain killer. So we read in Proverbs 31:6, "Give strong drink to him who is perishing, and wine to those who are bitter of heart." Anybody who has ever had too much to drink can tell you about the numbing effect of alcohol!

Finally, alcohol was used as an antiseptic or germ killer. That is why we read in the New Testament that the good Samaritan poured oil and wine on the wounds of the man who had been beaten by thieves. The fact is, when poured on a wound, alcohol can be a tool in the hands of God to destroy germs and bring healing. But when too much is poured into the human body, it can become a satanic poison that ruins a life.

THE MOST "SOBERING" LESSON I CAN TEACH MY KIDS

Now we come to the crux of the issue: what is the best policy to follow and, more to the point, what should we dads teach our kids concerning alcohol? It really is quite simple; there are only two choices: either we teach our kids to drink "only in moderation," or we teach them (and lead by example) *not to drink at all.*

I want to say respectfully, but firmly, to every moderate drinker reading this chapter: In my estimation, moderation is not the answer to the alcohol problem, but *a major cause of it.*

Two hundred years ago, Dr. Benjamin Rush said, "Many persons are destroyed by alcohol who were never completely intoxicated during the whole course of their lives." Recent research has shown that 72 percent of alcohol-related health problems, 67 percent of alcohol-related marital problems, 63 percent of alcohol-related violence, 58 percent of alcohol-related employment problems, and 55 percent of alcohol-related accidents and legal problems are caused by light and moderate drinkers.

Studies by the National Institute on Alcohol Abuse and Alcoholism indicate that 21 percent of even moderate drinkers become "psychologically dependent" on alcohol; that is, they think they need it. Yet another 14 percent are "symptomatic drinkers," meaning they are physically dependent and have difficulty in controlling their drinking.[23]

It has been stated that one ounce of alcohol kills ten thousand brain cells. No wonder William Shakespeare said, "Oh God, that men would put an enemy in their mouth to steal away their brain."

A woman once asked Thomas Edison, "Why don't you drink liquor?" Edison replied, "To take alcohol into the body is like putting sand on the bearings of an engine. It just doesn't belong. I have a better use for my brain than to poison it with alcohol." It is becoming increasingly clear that the consumption of alcohol, in any amount, is harmful in the long run.

Professor E. Don Nelson, of the University of Cincinnati School of Medicine, concluded on the basis of the latest research that "the less we drink the better off we are." He noted that, in any amount, alcohol kills cells in every organ of the body. Consequently, alcohol in any amount "causes permanent brain damage, primarily to the outer layers of the cortex, which governs complex thinking."[24]

Perhaps you have heard the story of two men who were talking, and one man said, "When I drink, I drink vodka because people cannot smell it on my breath, and therefore they don't know that I have been drinking." His friend said, "If I were you, I would drink something else, for it would be better for people to know that you are drinking than to think that you are stupid!"

These are not the only health problems associated with drinking "in moderation." Recent statistical studies, for example, have established a direct relationship between moderate use of alcohol and breast cancer. In one study, consumption of only two-thirds of a can of beer per week increased the risk by 40 percent; three drinks per week by 50 percent; and more than three drinks per week by 60 percent.[25]

Writer Leonard Gross summarized all of the recent research on this problem like this:

> Over the last fifteen years, the number of researchers in the United States and abroad have developed the proposition that what passes for social drinking today in many parts of the world is fraught with biomedical hazards, among them: liver problems including cirrhosis, hypertension, cancer of the digestive tract . . . fetal damage even before confirmation of pregnancy, and the impairment of sober intellectual capacities.[26]

Dad, keep this in mind: The only place the alcoholic can come from is the moderate drinker. It is a fact that one out of every twelve people who ever take a drink will become an alcoholic or a problem drinker. The fact is, you may not be one out of the twelve—but one of your children may be. Is it worth the risk?

I read something interesting recently about prohibition that made me sit straight up in my chair. Prohibition is widely condemned today as a national failure, and I know that it will never become national law again. But listen to the truth about this national experiment on banning alcohol. William Bennett said, "One of the clear lessons of prohibition is that when we had laws against alcohol there *was* less consumption of alcohol, less alcohol-related disease, fewer drunken brawls, and a lot less public drunkenness. Contrary to myth, there is no evidence that prohibition caused big increases in crime."[27]

The real facts are these: As a result of prohibition, 180,000 saloons were shut down, and 1,800 breweries went out of business. In ten years of prohibition, the death rate due to liquor decreased 42 percent, the death rate due to cirrhosis of the liver decreased 50 percent, the consumption of alcohol decreased by 70 percent, crime decreased 54 percent, and insanity decreased 66 percent.

My point? *What worked nationally will work in the home.* Whatever benefits derive from drinking (none of which I can call to mind) are far outweighed by the potential risk and actual cost. Remember, Solomon's purpose in writing Proverbs was to help his children "wise up in a dumbing down world." He flatly said, "whoever is led astray by [wine and strong drink] *is not wise"* (Prov. 20:1).

Just as discretion is the better part of valor, abstinence is the better part of wisdom. Alcohol and wisdom simply don't mix.

EXPERIENCE IS A POWERFUL TEACHER

My own dad was formerly a problem drinker. My family can share firsthand the tears, sorrow, and heartache alcohol leaves in its path. When my oldest brother, Richard, was about six years old, he went through a period of spasmodic, spontaneous outbursts of fear. He would be playing outside and all of a sudden rush into the house, crying hysterically and saying, "Mother, I am going to die. Please help me!" He slept fitfully and lost his appetite, and my parents finally took him to the doctor.

After an examination, the doctor excused him and asked my parents into his office. He began by assuring them that there was nothing *physically* wrong with their son and then asked, "Are there any problems at home?" My dad dropped his head in shame, and my mother refused to comment. The doctor said, "I will not pry, but there is a problem which is devastating your son emotionally and psychologically, and if you don't solve it, your son is in deep trouble."

My dad knew there was only one problem—his constant drinking. The Lord convicted my dad, and he knew he had a choice to make—his alcohol or his son's health. Not long after that Dad committed his life to Christ and instantly and totally gave up his drinking. Almost simultaneously my brother's outbreaks stopped, his appetite returned, and he was just another happy, playful boy.

I admit that my family got off much easier than many families plagued by alcohol. I could fill up an entire book with real life stories on the acid rain of grief, heartache, and devastation that has fallen on marriages, children, and families from the putrid trough of alcohol.

So I appeal to you, my fellow dads: Hear me as you consider this issue and determine carefully what you are going to teach your kids, both by example and precept, concerning the drinking of alcohol. As you ponder your decision, I want you to keep two words in mind: *influence* and *witness*.

The apostle Paul wisely stated, "It is good neither to eat meat *nor drink wine* nor do anything by which your brother stumbles or is offended or is made weak" (Rom. 14:21). My three sons are also my Christian brothers. One of the reasons why I am grateful that, by the grace of God, I have never taken a drink is that they can never use me as an excuse to begin drinking themselves.

Dad, meditate on this: 82 percent of teenagers will say yes to alcohol if their parents drink, but 72 percent of teenagers will say no to alcohol if their parents say no as well.[28] That is *influence!*

Let me ask you a question, fellow dad, and be completely honest. If you had your choice and the decision were yours to make, would your children eventually drink, or would they never touch alcohol at all? I believe any dad who would answer the former rather than the latter is either ignorant or plain dishonest. Assuming you would give the wise (and obvious) answer, some of you may need to put this book down, go to your refrigerator, cooler, cellar, or cabinet, and take your beer, wine, and/or liquor and make wise use of your kitchen sink. (If you do so, make sure your kids see you do this—it will be a great object lesson.)

But also think of the word *witness*. First Corinthians 10:31 says, "Therefore, whether you eat or drink, or whatever you do, do all to the glory of God." Everything you are to take into your body should be for the glory of God and for His pleasure. No Christian can say with a straight face (or a clear conscience) that he can drink what is the biblical equivalent of strong drink to the glory of God.

I will not deny the fact of Christian liberty. I know I cannot produce one verse that says, "Thou shall not drink." But there is not enough pleasure in one sip nor one toast to justify the possibility of causing a weaker brother to stumble, fall, or bring disgrace to the cause of Christ. (Just imagine what it would do to the image and witness of Billy Graham if he were seen drinking or on an ad smiling broadly with a beer in his hand and saying, "This Bud's for you!")

I know you are not Billy Graham. But you are a child of God (I hope), you have a sphere of influence, and you do bear witness for Christ, whether for good or for ill. I am hard pressed to think of any way that casual, social drinking can enhance your witness, much less bring people to Christ.

So, Dad, I am urging you as firmly as I can: Teach your children total abstinence from alcohol, and you be a total abstainer as well. General Robert E. Lee was correct when he said, "My experience through life has convinced me that abstinence from liquor is the best safeguard to morals and health."

BACK AWAY FROM THE CLIFF

I read a story recently of an ancient king who was seeking a driver for his chariot. Several men came to apply for the job. He asked each one this question: "If there were a cliff on one side of the chariot, how close could you drive to the edge?" The first man confidently answered, "I could drive within a foot of the edge." The second man said, "I could drive within six inches of the edge." The last man said, "Sire, I would drive just as far away from the edge as I possibly could." He got the job!

The best and safest decision we can all make concerning alcoholic beverages is to stay as far away from them as we possibly can.

In my opinion, Abraham Lincoln said it well and best when he declared, "Alcohol has many defenders, but no defense." Truer words were never spoken. This late, great president also made a resolution: "Whereas, the use of intoxicating liquors as a beverage is productive of pauperism, degradation, and crime; and believing it is our duty to discourage that which produces more evil than good, we therefore pledge ourselves to abstain from the use of intoxicating liquors as a beverage."[29]

Dad, would you not only join me in taking that pledge, but leading your children to do the same? I can assure you, with God as my witness, you will never regret it if you do.

Chapter 7

FISCAL FITNESS

*The trouble with the rat race is that
even if you win, you're still a rat.*

—Jane Wagner,
*The Search for Signs of Intelligent
Life in the Universe*

Y ou would expect that the wisest man and certainly one of
the richest who ever lived would have something to say
about money, and, in Solomon's case, you would be
right. There is a wealth of wisdom about wealth in Proverbs. With money, we find there is not only much to earn, but there
is much to learn!

In fact, the entire Bible has much to say about money. Howard
Dayton, the founder of Crown Ministries, has counted about 500
verses in the Bible on prayer, but more than 2,350 on how to handle
money and possessions.[1]

I know I can't label every chapter in a book "the most important," but this is certainly one of the most crucial in this book. The
ability to handle money today can (and does) make or break many a
family. A 1987 Gallup poll indicated that 56 percent of families consider economic problems the biggest challenge they face. The next
highest category is health problems and health care at only 6 percent.[2] Everybody seems to agree that money is unimportant—until

they don't have any! As Joe Lewis, the fighter, put it: "I don't like money actually, but it does calm my nerves."

WHO ARE THE WEALTHY?

Solomon refers often to "the wealthy" in Proverbs. Don't check out only because you think you may not fall into that category. The amount of hard cash lost each year in the United States amounts to about seventy-five dollars per capita, while the total average income for most of this planet comes to about sixty-nine dollars per person annually. In other words, the average American *loses* more money each year than almost anyone else in the world *earns*.[3] The average American is far more "wealthy" than he cares to admit.

Money is something we all live with and think we cannot live without. Money may come from *how* you make it, but money is *what* you make it, as this anonymous poem shows:

> Dug from the mountainside
>   or washing in the glen,
> Servant am I, or master of men.
> Earn me, I bless you;
>   steal me, I curse you!
> Grasp me and hold me,
>   a fiend will possess you.
> Lie for me, die for me,
>   covet me, take me—
>   angel or devil
> I'm just what you make me.[4]

Money is like nitroglycerin: Handling it is not morally wrong, but (especially if you do not know what you are doing) it is extremely risky! It seems as if everywhere you look, there is a warning label of some kind on toys, cigarettes, diet soft drinks, and even air bags. Perhaps it would be a good idea to put a warning label on dollar bills, certificates of deposit, and credit cards, for nothing has been the ruin of more people, marriages, and friendships than the failure to handle money properly.

Dad, next to teaching your child how to walk with God, you will never teach him a more important life lesson than how to handle money. I think it's safe to say that well over 90 percent of Americans have little clue on how to manage money. Again, like nitroglycerin, handling money can cause an explosion that can blow apart a marriage, a home, a business, and even a life. So, pay close attention to what the Word of God has to say.

HOW YOU MAKE IT IS WHAT YOU MAKE IT

The writer of Proverbs assumed that people will work to make money. In and of itself there is nothing wrong with making money. The Lord expects us to make money. Indeed, we read, "The blessing of the LORD makes one rich, and He adds no sorrow with it" (Prov. 10:22).

As Moses reminded the children of Israel, it is God who is the real "money maker." He said to them, "You shall remember the LORD your God, for it is He who gives you power to get wealth" (Deut. 8:18). Now, it stands to reason that if the Lord is the one who enables us to make money, then He expects us to earn money.

Yet Solomon tells us that there is a right way and a wrong way to make money. First, money should come by *hard work*, as the following verses show:

> He who has a slack hand becomes poor,
> But the hand of the diligent
>   makes rich. (Prov. 10:4)

> He who tills his land will be
>   satisfied with bread,
> But he who follows frivolity is
>   devoid of understanding. (Prov. 12:11)

Wealth gained by dishonesty will
    be diminished,
But he who gathers by labor will
    increase. (Prov. 13:11)

He who tills his land will have
    plenty of bread,
But he who follows frivolity will
    have poverty enough! (Prov. 28:19)

To labor, God says, "Give a good day's work." To management, God says, "Give a good day's wage." Both labor and management are to make money. Labor helps to make management a profit, while management helps labor make a salary. Neither a profit well earned nor a salary honestly made are displeasing to the Lord.

But money is also to be earned by *honest work.* There are grave warnings given to those who get their money dishonestly. There is a warning against *oppressing the poor.* "He who oppresses the poor to increase his riches, and he who gives to the rich, will surely come to poverty" (Prov. 22:16).

As I read this verse, I take comfort in the fact that one day the heat of God's fiery wrath will be felt by those who became millionaires by the addiction of the "poor" to drugs and alcohol. There is not a greater form of oppression than preying on the addiction of others to the "devil's brew."

There is also a warning about *cheating innocent people.* This can be done by charging excess interest on loans or artificially inflating prices. "One who increases his possessions by usury and extortion gathers it for him who will pity the poor" (Prov. 28:8).

A final warning is sounded about *dishonest business practices* like padding expense accounts. Listen to Eugene Peterson's translation of Proverbs 20:10: "Switching price tags and padding the expense account are two things God hates."[5]

God makes it plain: Winners never cheat, and He will see to it that cheaters never win.

Obviously, there are many more ways to gain money unethically and illegally. The point is, making money is expected and normal, but it must be made legitimately, morally, and ethically. Now, here is the rub (for most people): God is concerned with far more than the making of money. His greater concern is twofold: What do you do with money after you earn it, and—even more important—what does it do to you?

We began teaching our kids early these principles of industry, honesty, and responsibility. Here are a few methods we used which I recommend to you:

- Give your kids some jobs early on, without pay, such as making up their beds, picking up their toys, and cleaning their rooms. Inspect their room each time, encouraging them as much as possible, but also letting them know the standard of quality that is expected (no sloppy bed, toys left on the floor, etc.). This will begin to teach them the value of work, the fulfillment of doing a job well, and the discipline of following the commands of someone in authority over them.

- As your kids get older, choose some jobs they are capable of doing (polishing shoes, washing the car, vacuuming the floor, etc.) and settle on fair compensation. This will begin to instruct them in the value of money and reinforce the rewards of a job well done. Again, have an understood standard of quality that is expected and don't pay until the job is completed properly.

- Don't give allowances nor teach your children to expect them. Rather, teach them that money is earned through working for it. There is nothing wrong with giving your child money out of love or as a reward (such as for good grades), but kids must learn the relationship between honest labor and just compensation. In the next chapter, I will give you a sample "contract" you can use to help your children earn an "allowance."

Dad, the important thing to remember is that you are teaching values in the lives of your children that will last a lifetime. From school work to "home work," and as early as their toddler years, teach them that work is a part of life, that no one owes them anything, and money is to be primarily earned as fruit from the tree of honest labor.

WHO'S IN CHARGE—YOU OR YOUR MONEY?

You are either master over your money or a slave to it—there is no in between. As I walked through the rich grain fields of financial wisdom in Proverbs, I gleaned six keys to helping you master your money—lessons you can pass on to your children that will be "worth their weight in gold."

PRINCIPLE #1: BEING POOR IS A PROBLEM, BUT BEING RICH ISN'T THE ANSWER

The New Living Translation renders Proverbs 13:8 this way: "The rich can pay a ransom, but the poor won't even get threatened."[6]

The poor man may get no mail, but the rich man may get "blackmail!" For the rich, the bad news is that they are worth kidnapping. The good news is, they are able to pay the ransom. For the poor, the bad news is that they are not worth kidnapping. The good news is, they don't have to worry about ransom.

Solomon used this example to illustrate the real danger of money: Money solves problems, but it also creates them. In fact, it is the lust and desire for money that motivates the kidnapper. Patrick Morley put it well: "Money is intoxicating. It is an opiate that addicts us as easily and completely as the iron grip of alcohol or narcotics. . . . Money enslaves men—it will work you till you die and, after it has conquered your poor soul, its haunting laughter can be heard howling through the chambers of hell."[7]

PRINCIPLE #2: REMEMBER THE DIFFERENCE BETWEEN "NEEDY" AND "GREEDY"

When it comes to cars, we have all heard that "speed kills." Well, when it comes to money, "greed kills." "So are the ways of everyone who is greedy for gain; it takes away the life of its owners" (Prov. 1:19). We Americans pledge allegiance to "One nation under God" and then often live as if we believe in "One nation under greed."[8]

A greedy man is just like the heroin addict: it takes a "hit" to satisfy him; but the effect soon wears off, and he needs another "hit." When John D. Rockefeller was the richest man in the world, he was asked by an employee, "Mr. Rockefeller, how much money is enough?" To which Rockefeller replied, "Just a little bit more, son, just a little bit more." A Greek sage once said, "To whom a little is not enough, nothing is enough." If you do not have enough right now, you probably never will.

Larry Burkett advises parents to let their children know (at an age deemed appropriate) the family's income, living expenses, taxes, and giving habits. This will not only help them develop a realistic attitude about expenses, thrift, and stewardship, but will also enable them to see why being content with the family's style of living is necessary.[9]

PRINCIPLE #3: FAMILY COMES BEFORE MONEY, BOTH IN THE DICTIONARY AND IN LIFE

"He who is greedy for gain troubles his own house, but he who hates bribes will live" (Prov. 15:27). Any man (or woman) who puts work, career, money, or possessions above family is asking for big trouble. At one time, J. Paul Getty owned an estate that exceeded $4 billion in net worth. He was considered, in his day, the richest and most "successful" man on planet Earth. Years ago, the *Los Angeles Times* quoted something Getty wrote in his autobiography:

> I have never been given to envy, save for the envy I feel toward those people who have the ability to make a marriage work and endure happily. It's an art I have never been able to master. My record: five marriages, five divorces. In short, five failures.

The *Times* article continued:

> He termed the memories of his relationship with his five sons "painful." Much of his pain has been passed on with his money. His most treasured offspring, Timothy, a frail child born when Getty was fifty-three, died in 1958 at the age of twelve, of surgical complications after a sickly life, spent mostly separated from his father who was forever away on business.
>
> Other members of the Getty family also suffered from tragic circumstances. A grandson, J. Paul Getty III, was kidnapped and held for a ransom of $2.9 million. When Getty refused to pay, they held the boy for five months and eventually cut off his right ear. Getty's oldest son apparently committed suicide amid strange circumstances. Another son, Gordon Paul Getty, has been described as living a tortured existence. He was ridiculed in correspondence by his father and was the least favored son. Similar sorrow has followed other members of this unfortunate family.[10]

I am not trying to imply that being rich guarantees family problems, nor do I believe that every wealthy person has sacrificed his family to become so. I am simply saying that Solomon was right when he said that putting money first and family second can make you nothing more than a wealthy failure.

Dad, whenever possible, attend that child's ball game, recital, or school event. Let your children know early and often both in word and deed where your priorities are and where they are on that list.

PRINCIPLE #4: BE SATISFIED WITH NEEDS, NOT CONSUMED WITH WANTS

In the brilliant section of Proverbs penned by the mysterious Agur, we find a prayer loaded with financial wisdom.

Two things I request of You
(Deprive me not before I die):
Remove falsehood and lies far from me;
Give me neither poverty nor riches—
Feed me with the food allotted to me;
Lest I be full and deny You,
And say, "Who is the LORD?"
Or lest I be poor and steal,
And profane the name of my God. (Prov. 30:7–9)

Agur did not want to be either in the upper class or the lower class. He only wanted to be "middle classed." He didn't want to drive a Rolls Royce, and he didn't really want to walk; he only wanted a good used car!

I would venture to say that, in his own way, Agur was a rich man. He was like a man I heard of who lived on a very modest income. This man was talking one day to one of the big business tycoons who owned his company, a greedy, grasping businessman who was always trying to get more and more. They were sitting together at a lunch, and the employee looked at him and said, "I am richer than you are."

With a sneer, the tycoon said, "How do you figure that?"

The laborer said, "Because I have all the money I want, and you don't."

You can be rich in one of two ways: either in how much you have or how little you want. The debt crisis we have in this country (which we are going to explore momentarily) is primarily caused by greed and covetousness, which is simply the failure to be satisfied with enough. When you kill the tumor of greed, you destroy the cancer of covetousness.

Every Christmas in our church we put on an event called "Caring for Gwinnett" (Gwinnett is the county where our church is located). We invite the needy in our community to come to a free meal, present the gospel to them, and then treat their children to Christmas gifts our church people have generously bought. This past year we fed more than one thousand people and gave away more than two thousand gifts. As our children have witnessed this through the years, they have come away with a heightened appreciation of how blessed they are.

I encourage you dads periodically to involve your children in some type of project for needy people such as this, not only to teach them compassion but to help them to be more content with what they have. It is true that you never truly realize how much you have until you see how much others don't have.

PRINCIPLE #5: MONEY WILL NEVER TOTALLY SATISFY YOUR DEEPEST NEEDS OR EVEN ALL OF YOUR WANTS

You might think that people would naturally become happier as a culture becomes more affluent and wealthier, but consider this:

> In 1957, as John Galbraith was about to describe us as *the affluent society*, our per-person income, expressed in today's dollars, was less than $8,000. Today it is $16,000, making us The Doubly Affluent Society. Compared to 1957, we have twice as many cars per person; we have microwave ovens, color TVs, VCRs, air conditioners, answering machines, and $12 billion a year worth of brand-name athletic shoes.
>
> So are we happier than we were thirty-five years ago? We are not. In 1957 thirty-five percent of Americans told *The National Opinion Research Center* they were "very happy." In 1991, with doubled American affluence, thirty-one percent said the same. Judged by soaring rates of depression, the quintupling of the violent crime rate since 1960, the doubling of the divorce rate, the slight decline in marital happiness among the marital survivors, and the tripling of the teen suicide rate, we are richer and *un*happier. How can we avoid the shocking conclusion: Economic growth in affluent countries gives little boost to human morale.[11]

Dad, neither you nor your children will ever learn a greater lesson than this (if you have not learned it already): Money is not guaranteed to make you happier; in fact, it may make you sadder!

I constantly affirm to my children that my happiest times are simply when we are together. Dad, after you have rented that video, popped the popcorn, and enjoyed the fire or decorated the tree, take the opportunity to tell your kids that the experience you shared and the memories you built are far more valuable to you than a bigger bank account, a higher position, or any other material blessing.

PRINCIPLE #6: OVERTIME IS NOT WORTH IT OVER TIME

> Do not overwork to be rich;
> Because of your own
>   understanding, cease!
> Will you set your eyes on that
>   which is not?
> For riches certainly make
>   themselves wings;
> They fly away like an eagle
>   toward heaven. (Prov. 23:4–5)

To put this verse another way:
    Money talks, I'll not deny
    I heard it once, it said, "Good-bye."

The security of money is a mirage. Elvis Presley's stepbrother, Rick, is a dear friend of mine. The first time we met years ago, he told me the number one question people would ask him after Elvis died was this: "How much did Elvis leave behind?"

Rick just flashed that wide-faced, show-stopping grin of his and said, "James, you know what I tell them? 'He left it all.'"

I don't care how much money you make, how much money you save, how much money you invest, and how much money you keep. Eventually, either your money will leave you, or you are going to leave your money. So, Dad, never motivate your child to make the making of money his number one goal in life—he just might do it!

MERRITT'S METHODS OF MONEY MANAGEMENT (WITH A MONEY "BACK" GUARANTEE)

Managing money is not so much a matter of smarts as it is obedience and sanctified common sense. You don't have to be a Wall Street broker or a financial swami to manage money. I want to give you what I call "Merritt's Methods of Money Management." They are all based on the counsel of a king who saw everything he touched turn to gold.

From the time I married up to the present day, I have followed four simple rules in managing money, all based in the Book of Proverbs. I have tried to follow them consistently, and I know they work. If you follow these rules, you will ensure that you manage your money rather than your money managing you:

1. BELIEVE THAT GIVING IS MORE IMPORTANT THAN GETTING—THEN GIVE

Solomon went against the grain of all financial thinking when he said, in effect, that the key to getting is not getting but giving:

> Honor the LORD with your possessions,
> And with the firstfruits of all your increase;
> So your barns will be filled with plenty,
> And your vats will overflow with new wine.
> (Prov. 3:9–10)

Keep in mind that Proverbs was written to an agrarian culture. The income of the readers was tied to crops and livestock. Whenever a farmer or a rancher reaped a harvest or birthed some calves, he would take the first sheaf of the harvest or the firstborn of the flock and commit it to the temple and unto the Lord. In fact, the firstborn of his children also were committed to the service of the Lord. These were called "firstfruits."

By doing this, he was acknowledging God's goodness and God's sovereignty. In other words, by committing the firstfruits first to the Lord, the farmer was in effect confessing that all he had came from God and it all belonged to God. God demands first place in every area of our lives. The firstborn child would learn by this experience the place that God held in the family—what an object lesson!

When a person gives God the "first cut" of his money, he is acknowledging that God is first in this area of his life. This in turn gives confidence that God will provide for the basic necessities of life (v. 10). There is not a more important money-management principle you will ever hear than this one: Give God the "firstfruits," not the leftovers.

Mark Demoss is a dear friend who is a member of my church. His father, Arthur Demoss, was a spiritual giant and benefactor who gave millions to God's work and left behind a foundation to carry on his legacy. Mr. DeMoss said that to be successful you should give God the first dime out of every dollar, the first hour out of every day, and the first day out of every week. Dad, that is great advice for any father to pass along to his children.

Unfortunately, as wealthy as Americans are, God mostly gets the leftovers—and with many people, He doesn't even get the crumbs! Households earning $100,000 a year in 1990 gave on average 2.9 percent of their income to charity, while households with incomes of less than $10,000 gave 5.5 percent.[12]

What is even sadder is that as America becomes more prosperous, she's also becoming more stingy. In 1933, at the depth of the Great Depression, church members gave an estimated 3.3 percent of their disposable income to the church. If this trend continues, church members will be giving a scant 1.94 percent of their disposable income to the church by the year 2000.[13]

I read a story recently of a man named Gangaram Mahes. He is a criminal but a most extraordinary one. Although he has been arrested nearly three dozen times, you would never be frightened by his presence—that is, unless you own a classy restaurant.

He is known in New York as the "Serial Eater." This immigrant from Guyana loves eloquent dining but doesn't have the budget to pay for it. Rather than deny his appetite, he simply walks into a fine restaurant, orders the best meal on the menu, the finest liquors, and the most expensive desserts. He then eats and drinks to his heart's content, and, when the check arrives, simply informs the waiter he is neither able nor willing to pay the bill. The police then come and arrest him, and he ends up with at least a few days of free meals in jail.[14]

Our churches are filled with people who drink the milk of God's blessing, eat the steak of God's goodness, and enjoy the dessert of God's love—then won't even "tip" God 10 percent!

I am not saying that if you give money to God, God will give even more money back to you. He is not a heavenly slot machine that guarantees a jackpot every time you put "a coin" in the offering plate. But He does promise He will bless you far more abundantly than you would ever have dreamed possible if you will be faithful to Him financially. It may be with good health, favor with your boss, wisdom in financial decisions, a loving family, or a good job. It may even be with an eternal reward that you will never see this side of heaven, but you cannot outgive God.

Dad, I believe in tithing and have practiced it with the first dollar I ever made, selling crabapples from my Grandmother's backyard. I encourage you to urge, perhaps even insist, that from the first money your child earns he gives the "firstfruits" to the Lord. Also, let *him* give it. Let him put his money in the giving envelope, put it in the offering receptacle, and show him the church's financial statement recording his personal contribution. This not only teaches the child the duty of stewardship, but the joy of giving.

2. CASH OUT OR YOU WILL CASH IN

What does this principle mean? Well, put another way: Except for a house, a car (maybe), or an absolute emergency, *pay cash or don't buy it.* There are too many people for whom finances have become a matter of "life and debt." Today people can be divided into three classes:

1. The Haves

2. The Have-Nots

3. The Have-Not-Paid-for-What-They-Haves

Americans are the most indebted people on earth, with household debt averaging $71,500—twice that of Great Britain and eighty-nine times that of Switzerland.[15]

Recently there was a front page article in *USA Today* titled, "Rising Tide of Debt: Consumers Getting in over Their Heads with Credit Cards." It described the debt binge in America:

- Credit card debt has grown 20% a year since 1992.

- Total credit offered to consumers by bank card issuers is up 33% in one year, to $1.02 trillion.

- Consumers owe lenders a record 19% of their disposable income—not including mortgage and home equity loans, or auto leases. Credit-card debt alone is 7.5%.

- The average cardholder carries a balance of $3,900, only about a third pay their credit-card bills in full each month.[16]

The credit card boom has triggered the creation of a self-help group called "Big Spenders Anonymous for Compulsive Debtors."[17]

Yet what we call "credit" is not credit at all; it is really the opposite. For example, suppose you wanted to buy a refrigerator from an appliance store. You don't have the money right now, but the owner agrees to let you drop by once a month and pay one hundred dollars toward the price. He keeps the refrigerator but doesn't charge you any interest rate or lay away fee. When the refrigerator is paid for, it's yours.

Every time you pay one hundred dollars, you come away with a receipt showing a *credit* toward the purchase price. Your account is *credited* once a month, and when the *credit* paid equals the purchase price, the refrigerator is yours. Now *that* is credit.

But what society calls "credit" is really "debt." A "credit line" of one thousand dollars is actually a "debt potential" for that amount. So when you are buying something on "credit," you are actually buying it "on debt." It would be better to call a "credit card" a "debt card."[18]

I see bumper stickers frequently that read "I owe, I owe, so off to work I go!" I have a feeling that the message is more serious than it is funny. I am reminded of a handyman who had been called out to a millionaire's mansion to refinish her floors. The woman of the house said, "Be especially careful of this dining room table. It goes back to Louis XIV."

The handyman said, "Lady, don't feel bad. If I don't make a payment by Friday, my whole living room set goes back to Sears the sixteenth."

Someone has described a modern American as a person who drives a bank-financed car, over a bond-financed road, on gasoline he bought with a credit card, to a department store to get another charge account open so he can fill his house that is mortgaged to the Savings and Loan Association, with furniture that has been purchased on an installment plan!

Having said that, understand that the Bible does not condemn debt; the Bible *cautions* about debt. Solomon makes an oft-quoted statement about borrowing money that is often misunderstood and misused: "The rich rules over the poor, and the borrower is servant to the lender" (Prov. 22:7).

Contrary to popular opinion, this verse does not condemn debt, it merely states a fact. The borrower is a servant to the lender by the fact that he is bound to pay the lender what he owes him. He has an obligation he must fulfill. He has to pay what he owes. It is not wicked to borrow money; it is wicked to borrow money *and not repay it.* As Solomon's father said, "The wicked borrows and does not repay" (Ps. 37:21).

Incidentally, if your kids ever want to "borrow money," perhaps against a future allowance or a future chore to be done, let them (if it is for a good reason). But write down the terms of the agreement; when the money is to be repaid; and the penalty for a "late payment" (unless there are extenuating circumstances, such as illness). This will help them learn the real world of borrowing and the discipline of repaying debt on a timely basis.

Still, there are circumstances where I believe debt is wrong. I want to give you the following conditions when, if any or all are met, debt is indeed wrong and should be avoided:

- Debt is wrong when it is beyond your ability to repay it on a timely basis.

- Debt is wrong when it prevents you from giving to God what is right.

- Debt is wrong when the burden is so heavy you cannot save for the future.

- Debt is wrong if it puts your family under financial pressure. (Financial counselor Larry Burkett says that credit is the motivating factor behind perhaps 80% of all divorces.)[19]

- Debt is wrong if it is used to pay for the luxuries of life.

- Debt is wrong if it is generated by cosigning a note (see Prov. 6:1–6; 11:15; 17:18; 22:26–27).

As a rule of thumb, keep this in mind: It is all right to borrow for *necessities*, but you should pay cash for *luxuries*. So, if at all possible, *pay cash or don't buy it.*

A great way to teach your children this principle is to have them buy something they want with money they earn. It doesn't have to be much (perhaps ten dollars to buy a musical tape). Then let them buy it with their own money, impressing them with the fact that the thing bought is totally theirs and they owe no one.

3. SAVE FOR THAT RAINY DAY

Consider the ant who "provides her supplies in the summer, and gathers food in the harvest" (Prov. 6:8). The ant is always getting ready for the winter months when no work can be done. If only people had that much ant sense! I was astonished to read that eighty-five out of one hundred Americans end up with less than $250 in cash savings when they reach sixty-five.[20]

Can you believe that America's savings per household is $4,201—less than *one-third* that of Germany and less than *one-tenth* that of Japan?[21] Any fool can spend money—the wise man saves some as well.

One man had been sitting at a calculator for about three hours, not saying a word. Finally, he looked up and said to his wife, "Honey, if we continue to save at our present rate, by the time I retire we are going to owe $700,000." Keep in mind that *debt is the opposite of savings.* The reason is simple: *You either earn interest or you pay interest.* Savings earn interest, debt pays interest.

I know it is difficult for many families to save, but I want to encourage you to begin right now. The fact is, if we got by with less today, we could save up more for tomorrow.

One of the most fruitful methods we used with our children was this. Several years ago when our kids started earning an allowance, we gave them three jars. One was labeled "Saving," one "Spending," and one "Giving." They were required to set aside 10 percent for saving, at least 10 percent for giving, and the rest for spending.

It was our way of teaching our children the basic uses of money, the habit of wisely managing money, and in effect budgeting their money as they used the "spending" money to buy luxuries we would not pay for (CDs, magazines, etc.). My two oldest sons, James and Jonathan, now have part-time jobs and though they do not use the jars anymore, they still save, give, and oh yes—spend!

4. DON'T KEEP UP WITH THE JONESES

"There is one who makes himself rich, yet has nothing; and one who makes himself poor, yet has great riches" (Prov. 13:7). Will Rogers said, "People borrow money they don't have, to buy things they don't need, to impress people they don't even like." How true.

You can be spared a lot of sleepless nights and anxiety if you will just learn that not only should you refuse to keep up with the Joneses, but if you ever *do* catch up with them, they will just refinance! You will never be satisfied with what you have until you learn to be satisfied with what others have—that you don't.

THE BOTTOM LINE

Solomon was a "bottom line" kind of guy. You can sum up all that he had to say about money with these three statements:

1. *What you are is more important than what you have.* "Better is the poor who walks in his integrity than one perverse in his ways, though he be rich" (Prov. 28:6).

2. *What God sees in you is more important than what you have.* "Better is a little with the fear of the LORD, than great treasure with trouble" (Prov. 15:16).

3. *What others think of you is more important than what you have.* "A good name is to be chosen rather than great riches, loving favor rather than silver and gold" (Prov. 22:1).

There is nothing wrong with having things money can buy, as long as you don't lose the things that money can't buy. Never forget that money can buy anything that is for sale, but the greatest things in life are not for sale.

Take this little quiz to see how much you have learned from this chapter (then give this quiz to your kids). Who is richer?

- The crooked millionaire whose conscience is so guilt-ridden he cannot sleep; or the truck driver with a clear conscience who sleeps like a baby?

- The tycoon who is a cheat, womanizer, liar, and drunk, who only has "friends" he can buy; or the humble farmer who is a faithful husband, devoted father, and honest citizen, respected and loved by all who know him?

- The millionaire drug-baron on his way to hell; or the minimum wage worker on his way to heaven?

Dad, start with your kids when they are young and help them to see, spend, and save money wisely. A wise person observed that there are seven ages of man:

First age: A child sees the earth.
Second age: He wants it.
Third age: He hustles to get it.
Fourth age: He decides to be satisfied with about
    half of it.
Fifth age: He would be satisfied with less than half
    of it.
Sixth age: He is now content to possess a two-by-six
    foot section of it.
Seventh age: He gets it.[22]

Your children are at the first or the second age. Before long, they will enter the third and fourth age. Dad, if you can, accelerate them through those ages and get them as quickly as you can to the sixth age, because before they know it, they will be at the seventh age.

Socrates was looking around the marketplace that contained almost anything an Athenian of his day could want. At the end of his exploration he made this observation: "What a lot of things there are a man can do without."[23]

Fellow fathers, there are a lot of things a man can do without, and great wealth is one of them. What he cannot do without is peace with God, a family filled with love, a lifelong friendship with his kids, and a life well lived for the glory of God.

There is a great cost to money, and oftentimes the price is too high to pay. So, Dad, if you want to be "fiscally fit," put God first, family second, church third, money a distant fourth, let God give you what you need, and be satisfied with what you have. You will not only die a happy man; but if you can pass these truths along to your kids you will be a successful father.

Chapter 8

MANUAL LABOR IS NOT THE PRESIDENT OF MEXICO

It's true hard work never killed anybody,
but I figure, why take the chance?

—Ronald Reagan

T wo teenagers were talking, and one said to the other, "I'm really worried. Dad slaves away at his job so I will never want for anything, pays all of my bills, and sends me to college. Mom spends every day washing and ironing and cleaning up after me, and even takes care of me when I am sick."

"So, what are you worried about?" his puzzled friend asked.

"I'm afraid they might try to escape!" he replied.

That story reflects my belief that Americans have succeeded in making baby busters and "Generation X" perhaps the most spoiled generations in American history. Many young people (and adults unfortunately) really do think Manual Labor is the president of Mexico. Hard work is too often seen as a great evil. And where welfare was once a dirty word, it has now taken on the tag of "entitlement."

Our children (including my own, at one time) often feel they are "entitled" to an allowance and see parents as human ATMs with the code word "Give-Me." Some young people even get the idea that if they are made to work it is somehow un-American.

One young lady, trying to be a little hip, walked up to her dad and said, "Dad, can I have some mun to hit the flick?" (Translation: May I have some money to go to the movies?)

Her dad looked at her and said, "No, you cannot have any 'mun to hit the flick.' But you can 'swish the dish, spread the bed, and flop the mop!'"

Solomon would have resonated with that dad's response, for as we will see, he was extremely opposed to laziness. At all costs, he did not want his children to become *sluggards* (a word seldom used today that describes a lifestyle very much in vogue). We, too, should be concerned since our children will spend one-half the waking hours of their prime adult life working.

LEISURE ISN'T THE PROBLEM

It should be noted that Solomon had no problem with leisure. Every laborer needs leisure, for a laborer rested and refreshed will be a better laborer. The contrast in Proverbs is between labor and laziness.

Work, contrary to some thinking, is not a dirty word. The way some people treat it, you would think it is obscene. I have even heard some Bible teachers and preachers misinterpret work as a curse that came as a result of the fall of Adam and Eve. Nothing could be further from the truth.

This world is the result of God's work (Gen. 2:2). God gave Adam the job of tending the garden of Eden before sin came on the scene (Gen. 2:15). God's own Son was a carpenter (Mark 6:3). Paul, one of the greatest Christians in history, was a tentmaker (Acts 18:1–3).There is nothing dishonorable about work worth doing and work done well.

President Theodore Roosevelt was right when he said, "Extend pity to no man because he has to work. If he is worth his salt, he will work. I envy the man who has work worth doing, and does it well. . . . far and away the best prize that life offers is the chance to work hard at work worth doing."[1]

Somehow we have lost the spirit, if not the letter of President Roosevelt's thinking. Ask any employer, and he will tell you that to find someone who will work, work hard, do the job right, and finish the task, is as rare as public prayer in a public school (that's another topic for another discussion).

Dad, I believe one of the best things you can do for both the character and the reputation of your children is to pass on to them a strong work ethic, and warn them of the dangers of laziness.

IT'S NOT THAT HE'S LAZY— HE JUST WON'T WORK

When you read the Book of Ecclesiastes, you can't help but conclude in a hurry that, whatever faults Solomon had, one was not laziness! Solomon's favorite term for the lazy person is "sluggard." He uses the term no less than seventeen times in the Book of Proverbs. Please understand that the sluggard is not a person who would work but just cannot; the sluggard, rather, is a person who could work but will not.

A fellow went to the Welfare Office and applied for financial assistance. At the beginning of his interview an official asked, "Why do you need financial aid?"

"I'm having trouble with my eyes," the man replied.

The bureaucrat asked, "And what is the nature of your eye trouble?"

"I just can't see myself going to work," the man answered.

Every sluggard has the same "eye trouble." The sluggard's only on-the-job training is laziness. Work doesn't bother the sluggard—as long as someone else is doing it! As I perused the Book of Proverbs, I found five basic characteristics of the sluggard.

1. THE SLUGGARD LOVES SLEEP AND HATES ALARM CLOCKS

Indeed, the sluggard and sleep are so closely linked, Solomon gives no less than five warnings concerning the kind of sleep that crosses the line between rest and laziness. Has it ever occurred to you that there is a difference between getting enough rest and getting too much sleep? While proper rest is healthy for the body, excess sleep is harmful in more ways than one.

- Too much sleep has a dulling effect. "As a door turns on its hinges, so does the slothful turn on his bed" (Prov. 26:14). Excess sleep can become a hinge anchoring the body to the bed.[2]

- Too much sleep disables ambition. "Laziness casts one into deep sleep, and an idle person will suffer hunger" (Prov. 19:15).

- Too much sleep brings poverty. "Do not love sleep, lest you come to poverty" (Prov. 20:13a).

- Too much sleep disappoints God. "How long will you slumber, O sluggard? When will you rise from your sleep?" (Prov. 6:9).

- Too much sleep wastes golden opportunities. "He who gathers in summer is a wise son; he who sleeps in harvest is a son who causes shame" (Prov. 10:5).

Normally, the hard-working person gets up when he wakes up; but when the lazy person wakes up he just rolls over—as a door on its hinges. In other words, there is much motion but no progress.

One man was filling out a job application form that asked, "Does hard work bother you?" He answered, "Hard work does not bother me in the least. I can lie down next to it and go right to sleep." That is the sluggard!

His god is sleep, his bed is his altar, and his body is the sacrifice he willingly offers. The sluggard is the ultimate couch potato. He can do anything as long as he is "lying down on the job."

Dad, to help your children conquer the alarm clock, have an agreed upon period of time they can sleep. Keeping in mind that younger kids do need more sleep, expect your kids to go to bed at a reasonable hour so that they can rise earlier. Have a rule that the "snooze button" is off limits. Enforce the discipline that when they wake up, they get up!

On days they are not in school (such as Saturday) have them finish any chores early in the day so the meat of the day can be given to enjoyable, leisurely activities. I often tell our boys something I learned from my dear friend Zig Ziglar: "When you do what you have to do when you have to do it, then you can do what you want to do when you want to do it."

2. FROM START TO FINISH, THE SLUGGARD RARELY STARTS AND NEVER FINISHES

Amazingly, a sluggard will go hungry before he will work. We have been taught to feed the hungry, and we should feed those who are truly hungry and cannot provide for themselves; but some people should be allowed to go hungry if their hunger is brought on by their own laziness. Solomon said, "Laziness casts one into a deep sleep, and an idle person will suffer hunger" (Prov. 19:15). Centuries later the apostle Paul was even more explicit: "For even when we were with you, we gave you this rule: 'If a man will not work, he shall not eat'" (2 Thess. 3:10, NIV).

The sluggard doesn't work and therefore makes no income; with no income he can buy no food and with no food he goes hungry. However, the problem does not stop there. Listen to what else Solomon says about the sluggard:

> The slothful man does not roast
>   what he took in hunting,
> But diligence is man's precious
>   possession. (Prov. 12:27)

> A lazy man buries his hand in
>   the bowl,
> And will not so much as bring
>   it to his mouth again. (Prov. 19:24)

The sluggard loves buttered bread, but he is too lazy to butter it himself. If he kills an animal, he won't even clean the meat and cook it. He not only wants someone else to cook his meal, he wants someone else to feed it to him! The point is, he never starts a job; and if you give him one, he either won't finish it or he will do it only half way.

We have always reviewed our sons' schoolwork to see to it that they are completing their assignments, turning in their homework in a timely fashion, and doing their best work. We reward good grades monetarily to reinforce a job well done. If we agree on "quality control" for a chore or other responsibility, and after fair warning the job is still unfinished or done poorly, they lose their reward.

As you will see later in the allowance "contract," if one of my sons leaves for school without his room clean, he forfeits that day's prorated portion of the allowance. We constantly reinforce the axiom that a job worth doing is worth doing well.

3. WHEN THE SLUGGARD SAYS LATER, HE MEANS NEVER

The sluggard is the master procrastinator. He never does today what he can put off until tomorrow, and he never does tomorrow what he can put off forever.

His favorite work day is tomorrow. That is why God is always asking him, "How long will you slumber, O sluggard? When will you rise from your sleep?" (Prov. 6:9). If you are continually asking a person, "How long are you going to take off between jobs?" or "When are you going to look for another job?" you are talking to a sluggard.

Perhaps you have heard about the college student who was trying to decide whether he should study. He grabbed a coin, flipped it, and in midair said, "Heads, I'm going to the movies; tails, I'm going to watch TV; if it stands on its edge, I'm going to study." Some sluggards are even too lazy to flip the coin! The sluggard is the person who is always going to "get around to doing the job," but he never "gets around" to "getting around."

When a job is to be started is as important as when it is to be completed. A child's favorite response to a command is often "in just a minute." Don't start buying it, or you will be paying for it forever. Teach your kids that "now" means now and "finish" means don't turn the TV back on until the job is done.

4. THE SLUGGARD IS A BIG DREAMER BUT A LITTLE DOER

"The desire of the lazy man kills him, for his hands refuse to labor" (Prov. 21:25). His favorite refrain is "One day . . . ." You can just hear him now:

"*One day* I am going to hit it big."

"*One day* I am going to settle down to one job."

"*One day* I am going to own my own business."

"*One day* I am going to hit the jackpot."

He wants what everybody wants—he just doesn't want to work for it. This thinking is one of the major reasons for the explosion of the welfare state. As Robert Hicks has wisely noted, "Feeling we're entitled to things without being willing to do the necessary labor to obtain them, makes us a society of sluggards."[3]

The American dream for some has become the American nightmare for others because of their refusal to work to make those dreams come true. Dad, don't give even your small children *everything*. When they want certain things you feel they should and could buy by doing chores, let them earn it and turn their dreams into reality.

5. THE SLUGGARD WORKS HARD— AT DEFENDING HIS LAZINESS

"The lazy man is wiser in his own eyes than seven men who can answer sensibly" (Prov. 26:16). There is one thing you will never convince the sluggard of: that he is a sluggard. Even if seven wise men tell him he is lazy, he will not admit it—no matter that he is outnumbered seven to one. You can tell a sluggard, but you can't tell him much.

125

He always has an excuse as to why he cannot work. That is the meaning of Solomon's statement: "The way of the lazy man is like a hedge of thorns, but the way of the upright is a highway" (Prov. 15:19). When the sluggard looks out the front door of life, he doesn't see a highway of opportunity; he only sees one big briar patch—or even a lion! "The lazy man says, 'There is a lion outside! I shall be slain in the streets!'" (Prov. 22:13; see also 26:13).

He sees a dark lining in every silver cloud, an obstacle in every opportunity. Though he cannot (will not) hold down a job, there is always a good excuse. The hours are too long; the pay is too little; the job is too hard; and the people are too demanding—take your pick. (Don't worry if you don't like any of those; he has plenty more. Did you hear the one about the lion?)

Solomon said, "The lazy man will not plow because of winter" (Prov. 20:4). It's always either too hot, too cold, too wet, or too dry to work. The point is, he always has an excuse. Thomas Edison, the epitome of a worker and the antithesis of a sluggard, said, "Opportunity is missed by most people because it is dressed in overalls and looks like work."[4] Old Benjamin Franklin was right when he said, "I never knew a man who was good at making excuses who was good at anything else."

The bottom line is, the sluggard would rather make excuses than make a living. He is an expert at doing nothing, calling it something, and defending it in the process.

Children have file cabinets full of excuses. I have had to tell my kids on a few occasions, "It's time you learned the world doesn't want excuses; it wants results. Give your excuses while you are doing the job."

IT'S CRAZY TO BE LAZY!

If the sluggard harmed only himself, it would be one thing. But the sluggard has a negative effect on society, his family, coworkers, and even grieves God Himself. Laziness has consequences that adversely affect everybody.

The sluggard represents *wasted talents*. "He who is slothful in his work is a brother to him who is a great destroyer" (Prov. 18:9). The tragedy of the sluggard is that he wastes the God-given abilities and gifts that are to be used not only to be productive but for the glory of his Creator.

What is worse, the lazy employee, besides being unproductive, is also destructive. He negatively affects an entire organization. As one writer astutely observed:

> That word "destroys" pulsates with liabilities. A lazy employee doesn't simply hold an organization back, he *destroys* its motivation and drive. A lazy player doesn't just weaken the team, he *destroys* its spirit and diminishes its will to win. A lazy pastor doesn't merely limit a church, he *destroys* its enthusiasm, its passion to win souls and meet needs. Before long, everyone must do more to compensate for the sluggard's negative influence.[5]

If you're a businessman, you know the truth of this statement: It is better to be shorthanded than to hire a sluggard; better to have nobody than a lazy body. Evidently, Solomon had suffered through a few sluggards on his payroll, for he said, "As vinegar to the teeth and smoke to the eyes, so is the lazy man to those who send him" (Prov. 10:26). Do you know how irritating vinegar is when taken straight, or how aggravating smoke is when it gets in your eyes? That's how irritating a lazy person is to the person who hires him.

Whatever he does will take twice as long to finish and will either have to be done over or thrown out—at twice the cost. His presence on the job is worse than his absence from it.

The sluggard also represents *wasted resources*. A tragic picture is painted in Proverbs 24:30–31:

> I went by the field of the lazy man,
> And by the vineyard of the man
>   devoid of understanding;
> And there it was, all
>   overgrown with thorns;

127

Its surface was covered with nettles;
Its stone wall was broken down.

With the sluggard, what could and should have been the Ponde-rosa will instead become Mr. Haney's farm on Green Acres. Where there should be a beautiful car with glistening chrome, clean windows, and spotless interior will instead be a rundown and rusted-out jalopy.

Worst of all, the sluggard represents *wasted living*. The slug-gard ultimately winds up in the soup line looking for handouts, not because he had to but because he chose to. Solomon's final warning to the sluggard is this:

A little sleep, a little slumber,
A little folding of the hands to rest;
So your poverty will come like a prowler,
And your want like an armed man.
(Prov. 24:33–34)

We are to have pity on the poor, but only on those who are poor because of oppression, disaster, health, or conditions beyond their control—not those who choose to be. Can I tell you what made Abra-ham Lincoln such a great man? It was not that he was born in a log cabin, but that he got out of it!

In 1758 these words were written in Poor Richard's Almanac: "Laziness travels so slowly, that Poverty soon overtakes him."[6] Tragically, it soon overtakes others as well. The poverty of the slug-gard—especially if the sluggard is a husband and a father—will over-take his family as well. His babies will go to bed hungry; his children will be ill-clothed in the winter; his family will never have a place they can call "home" because they must always be on the move from apartment to trailer to apartment; and the rent is never paid.

As a pastor, I am chagrined to say that I have met more than a few sluggards in the churches I have pastored. I believe Paul must have written, with a hand trembling with anger, these words: "But if anyone does not provide for his own, and especially for those of his household, he has denied the faith and is worse than an unbeliever" (1 Tim. 5:8). Do you want to avoid the title "worse than an unbeliever"? Then stay far away from the ways of the sluggard—and make sure that your kids do too.

THE WORTH OF WORK

How do we teach our kids the value and the virtue of work? Solomon's simple solution to slothfulness is study (try saying that three times rapidly!) You heard me right—study. Solomon took his children out to a pile of dirt one day and made them study—are you ready for this?—the ant.

> Go to the ant, you sluggard!
> Consider her ways and be wise,
> Which, having no captain,
> Overseer or ruler,
> Provides her supplies in the summer,
> And gathers her food in the harvest.
>   (Prov. 6:6–8)

That alone tells me how truly wise and brilliant Solomon was, for there is not a creature on earth that personifies a good work ethic more than the ant. (So take heart, dads. If your kids are "antsy," that ain't all bad!) Consider only a few of the ant's admirable qualities.

1. THE ANT IS A WORKER YOU CAN COUNT ON

While the queen ant is the center of attention and the mother of most of the ants in the colony, she is not the chief ruler. Instead, the work and survival of the colony is ensured by "soldier" ants. These servant leaders are older ants who begin each new activity in the colony by doing the work themselves. Younger ants then imitate the servant-leaders and join in the work. There are no supervisors, chiefs, or officers among the ants.[7] That explains Solomon's comment that ants have "no captain, overseer or ruler" (v. 7).

The ant is a self-starter, a picture of the diligent person described in Proverbs 10:4: "He has a slack hand becomes poor, but the hand of the diligent makes one rich." The diligent person in Proverbs is the opposite of the sluggard. The word *diligent* means "to cut or sharpen." It denotes the worker who is sharp, decisive, and keen. He wants to work, make a difference, and contribute to his family and society. What the ant does by instinct, humans should do by desire.

2. THE ANT STAYS ON TASK

The job of most ants is to find food so that the colony can eat. Their hunger naturally drives them to their job rather than to the welfare office (except ants don't have a welfare state; they either work or die). Again, the ant knows hunger is not all bad. As Solomon observed, "The person who labors, labors for himself, for his hungry mouth drives him on" (Prov. 16:26). Hunger is God's motivating force to labor. That stomach growl to the sluggard is God's way of saying, "Get a job and get a life!"

The ant never sees work as menial or beneath his dignity. Whether it is moving dirt or carrying bread crumbs, he merrily goes along doing his job. How unlike that are many people today! Someone has remarked that if you want to keep teenagers out of hot water, put dirty dishes in it!

Dad, one of the greatest lessons you will ever teach your kids is that all work is valuable. All work can, and should be done, for the glory of God. The sum of the matter is found in this simple statement: "In all labor there is profit." (Prov. 14:23).

One day your kids will decide what their life's "vocation" is going to be. As they make this crucial decision, you would do well to teach them that the very word *vocation* comes from the Latin word *vocare,* meaning "to call." Every vocation, regardless of what it is, is a calling from God.[8]

Martin Luther King Jr. rightly declared, "Not all men are called to specialized or professional jobs; even fewer to the heights of genius in the arts and sciences; many are called to be laborers in factories, fields and streets. But no work is insignificant."[9]

There is an old-fashioned word we use in our house called *chores.* Our kids get an allowance—but again, they get it the "old-fashioned way." They earn it. At our house my two younger sons *earn* an allowance. They have signed a contract. (I am big on those for several reasons. First, it clarifies expectations so there are no misunderstandings. Second, it teaches the importance of being careful of what you sign. Third, it teaches integrity and faithfulness in keeping your word.) The following is a sample contract with my two sons:

CONTRACT WITH CHARACTER

1. Daily chores

    a. daily devotions
    b. make up bed/clean room
    c. clean up bathroom of your towels, clothes, etc.
    D. be at breakfast at 7:30 A.M.

2. Do jobs asked with positive attitude.

3. Additional chores—Jonathan:

    a. vacuum study/dust study once a week
    b. dishwasher twice a week
    c. vacuum once every other week
    d. clean bathrooms once a month

4. Additional chores—Joshua

    a. collect garbage twice a week
    b. dishwasher twice a week
    c. vacuum once every other week
    d. clean bathrooms once a month

5. Allowance paid every Friday.

6. 10 percent tithe/10 percent savings/other money to be used wisely and with counsel of parents.

Signed: _____Jonathan Merritt

Signed: _____Joshua Merritt

Signed: _____Mom and Dad

3. THE ANT WORKS WHEN IT IS TIME TO WORK

As I have stated previously, the ant may be the hardest working creature on earth. Consider this: A leaf-cutting ant may carry up to fifty times its own weight more than a hundred yards. That is equivalent to a two-hundred-pound man carrying five tons on his back for a distance of seventeen miles. In a single summer, a large colony of ants may excavate thirty thousand to forty thousand pounds of earth to make its nest, and carry five thousand pounds of material back into the nest for food.[10]

The ant may make as many as four round trips a day to food sources, which may be more than four hundred feet from the nest. That is roughly equivalent to a man's walking sixty-eight miles. If the ant had the stride of a man, it would be capable of bursts of speed in excess of sixty-five miles an hour and would walk normally at a speed of twenty miles per hour.[11] (And you think you have it rough!) One thing about an ant you can always count on: he always gives his best and pulls his share of the load.

The ant has so much to teach us. Dad, instruct your kids that their reputation will never rise above their work ethic and how people see them as workers. My oldest son, James Jr. (seventeen), and my middle son, Jonathan (fourteen), are now workers. James works in our church doing maintenance, and Jonathan works for a man in our church doing yard work. People have paid me compliments about my sons before, but I don't think I have ever been prouder than when both of their "bosses" recently came to me, without any prodding, to tell me that my boys were hard workers who could be trusted to do a job well.

4. THE ANT FINISHES THE JOB

The ant literally dies working—and so should we. I have searched the Bible, and I have never found there the contemporary concept of retirement. You may retire from a *job*, but you never retire from *work*. As long as you are alive, there is always a work for God that He wants you to do.

You dads might want to share this with your fathers and grandfathers: "Harvard University commissioned a study of its graduates.

132

One group of one hundred men retired at age 65, those in the other group worked to age 75. In the first group, seven out of eight were dead by age 75. In the second (those who kept working) only one in eight had died. The researchers concluded that retiring too early reduces longevity."[12]

Dad, the greatest example of work you will ever find is the Lord Jesus Christ Himself, who said at the end of His three-year ministry: "I have finished the work which You have given Me to do" (John 17:3). Has it ever occurred to you that salvation is available because Jesus proved Himself to be a faithful laborer who stayed on task until the job was done? Teach your kids to do the same. They will be happier and so will you.

WHAT YOU DO, DO WELL

Everyone on my staff has a framed copy of the following saying by Walt Disney, which explains why only Disney World is Disney World: "Do what you do so well, that those who see you do what you do are going to come back to see you do it again, and tell others that they should see you do what you do."[13]

A tall order? You bet. But it works, it's biblical, and it's what we dads are called to do. Dad, whatever else you teach your kids about work, teach them to:

- Work hard
- Finish the job
- Do their best

If they learn that lesson well and put it into practice, you won't have to teach them much about success—because it will already be their close friend and constant companion.

Chapter 9

HOW TO DEAL WITH FRIENDS, FOES, AND FOOLS

I will pay more for the ability
to deal with people
than any other ability under the sun.

—John D. Rockefeller

R elationships: we all have them. John Donne was right: "No man is an island."[1] With few exceptions, success in life depends so much on the ability to establish and maintain proper relationships with the right people.

According to a report by the American Management Association, an overwhelming majority of the two hundred managers who participated in a survey agreed that the most important single skill of an executive was his ability to get along with people. Management rated this ability more vital than intelligence, decisiveness, knowledge, or job skills.[2]

Relationships can make your child or break your child (and you, for that matter). A true story illustrates graphically just how crucial our relationships are and how vital it is we choose to enter into the right ones.

Several years ago, two young women from southern California spent the day doing some last-minute Christmas shopping in Tijuana,

Mexico, a few miles south of San Diego. As they returned to their car, one of the ladies glanced down in the gutter and noticed something moving and squirming as if in terrible pain.

As they bent down, they noticed what appeared to be a dog—what they thought was a tiny Chihuahua—struggling for its life. It was breathing heavily, shivering, and almost dead. They felt so sorry for this little animal they couldn't just drive off and leave it there to die.

They decided to take it home with them and try to nurse it back to health. Since they were afraid that the little creature would be detected by the Board of Patrol Officers, they hid it in the trunk of their car. After they crossed the border, they stopped and one of the women took the little "Chihuahua" out and held it the rest of the way home.

Finally, they pulled up in front of the home of one of the ladies and decided she would keep the little animal through the night and try to help it regain its strength. She took it in the house and tried feeding it some of her food, but it wouldn't eat. She patted it, cuddled it, held it, talked to it, and finally wrapped it in a small blanket and placed it beneath the covers of her bed to sleep beside her all through the night. She kept feeling it to make sure it was OK.

Early the next morning, the animal was no better. She decided to take it to an emergency animal clinic nearby. She handed the weakened animal to the doctor on duty and began to describe all the things she had done to try to help nurse this "dog" back to life.

The veterinarian quickly interrupted her and asked, "Where did you *get* this animal?"

Seeing the look on his face and fearful of being reprimanded for bringing this animal across the border, she told him she was keeping it for a friend who had found it.

The doctor looked at her sternly and said, "I'm not letting you leave until you tell me where you got this thing."

She confessed, "Doctor, to be honest with you, my friend and I were shopping in Tijuana, and we found this little Chihuahua in the gutter near our car. We were just trying to nurse it back to health."

"Lady," the doctor replied, "this is no Chihuahua. What you brought home with you is a rabid Mexican river rat!"[3]

What these two women thought to be harmless turned out to be not only dangerous but deadly. How much truer is this of relationships? When it comes to our kids (and let's be honest, us adults too), peer pressure can be just as dangerous and twice as deadly.

According to Solomon, along life's way your children will encounter people of every ilk and sort. Some will become friends, others will become foes (even Jesus had enemies), and others will prove themselves to be fools.

Dad, you will do your children an incredible favor by teaching them both how to differentiate between these groups of people and how to relate to them with wisdom and personal skill. In this chapter I want to focus our attention on our relationships with our friends, for that is where we will spend most of our lives. I believe this relationship is the most crucial of all.

BE COMMITTED TO FRIENDS

Early on, our children need to learn how rare and valuable true friendship really is. Quite frankly, none of us makes very many true friends—at least, we better not! Solomon warns us, "A man of many friends comes to ruin" (Prov. 18:24, NASB). Nobody has many true friends, and it is risky to have too many "friends" because not every so-called friend will prove to be one, as Jeremiah warned King Zedekiah (Jer. 38:22). The wrong "friend" may betray you—as Judas proved with Jesus (though Jesus still called him "friend," see Matt. 26:50).

Nevertheless, as you journey along the path of life, one of the great treasures you find are the jewels of true friendship. Proverbs contains a treasure trove of divine wisdom in the area of friendships. Let's consider several of its most precious jewels.

I. BE A FRIEND

Solomon said, "A man who has friends must himself be friendly" (Prov. 18:24). If you want to have a friend, you must first be a friend.

I went out to find a friend
   but could not find one there;
I went out to be a friend,
   and friends were everywhere.

I am convinced that friendliness does not have to be limited by personality. Friendliness does not necessarily mean having an aggressive, dynamic personality, getting in everyone's face, and slapping them on the back, with words flowing ninety miles a minute. (Some of these "friends" act like such fools, you wish they were foes!)

I believe even the shy, quiet, and reserved individual can be taught to be friendly. You do not *take* friends; you *make* friends. The best way to find a good friend is to be a good friend. It is next to impossible to have no friends if you yourself are friendly. The opposite of that is also true.

Psychologists once asked a group of college students to jot down the initials of the people they disliked. Some of the students taking the test could think of only one person; others listed as many as fourteen. But the interesting fact that came out of the research was this: *Those who disliked the largest number of people were themselves the most widely disliked.*[4] You will find that the more likable you are, the more likely you are to like other people and to be liked by them.

One of the greatest lessons I have ever learned on how to be a friend came from a statement made by Dale Carnegie, the author of the best-seller *How to Win Friends and Influence People.* He said, "You can make more friends in two months by becoming interested in other people, than you can in two years by trying to get other people interested in you."

Being friendly is both a science and an art. It can be learned and improved with practice. If you will teach your children a few things early in life, it will carry them a long way in interpersonal relationships:

- Maintain eye contact. When you talk to people, look them in the eye.

- Smile! It takes seventy-two muscles to frown, only fourteen to smile, and a smile encourages conversation.

- Call people by their names. Strangers are just that, strange, but a friend is known.

- Talk to others about their favorite topics—themselves.

- Find an occasion to give a word of encouragement, compliment, or show an act of kindness.

You show me a person who practices and applies those five traits with whomever he comes in contact, and I will show you a person who has a reputation for being friendly.

2. CHOOSE A FRIEND WISELY

Let me give you a rule of thumb on friendship: *Be friendly to everyone, but don't have everyone as a friend.* Dad, urge your kids to heed this warning: "The righteous should choose his friends carefully, for the way of the wicked leads them astray" (Prov. 12:26). The word *choose* in the Hebrew is *tur* and is used most often in the Old Testament of a man searching out land. The wise person explores and evaluates prospective friendships, selects them prudently, and enters into them carefully.[5]

Benjamin Franklin once said, "Be slow in choosing a friend, and even slower in changing." That is excellent advice. It is important not only to choose friends but to reject the wrong friends. The reason one should choose his friends carefully is because "the way of the wicked leads them astray."

Two extremely wise men—one of history's greatest preachers, the other one of our nation's greatest presidents—made two observations our children would be wise to hear and remember:

> A man is known by he company he shuns, as well as by the company he keeps.—C. H. Spurgeon[6]

> Associate with men of good quality if you esteem your own reputation; for it is better to be alone than in bad company.—George Washington

It is fair to say that there are people in hell today because they chose the wrong friends. Our jails are filled with thugs who should have been college graduates contributing to society, but, instead, they ran with the wrong crowd. Mark it down: Listening to the wrong people, following the wrong advice, and emulating the wrong example is the sure result of wrong friendships.

A farmer was being troubled by a flock of crows in his cornfield. Deciding he'd had enough, he loaded his shotgun and crawled unseen along the fence row, determined to blow those crows out of the sky. Now, this farmer had a very "sociable" parrot who indiscriminately made friends with everybody.

Seeing the flock of crows, the parrot flew over and joined them, just trying to be sociable. The farmer saw the crows but didn't see his parrot. He took careful aim, fired, and then jumped up and ran over to see how many crows he had shot. Lo and behold, there was his parrot, lying on the ground with a broken wing and a chipped beak, but he was still alive.

The farmer tenderly picked up his parrot and brought him home, where the man's children ran out to meet him. Upon seeing their injured parrot, they tearfully asked, "Daddy, what happened?" Before he could answer, the parrot spoke up, "That's what you get for hanging out with the wrong crowd."

It is a truism that you can never be at the right place, at the right time, doing the right thing, if you are with the wrong crowd. Part of our responsibilities as dads is to help our kids run with the right crowd. This introduces the ticklish subject of the role we should play in the friendships our kids make and the company they keep.

It is important to understand here my personal vantage point. I was reared in a home where my dad had one rule: As long as I put my feet under his table, ate his food, slept under his roof, and lived in his house, *he* set the rules. There were clear guidelines of what was expected of me in terms of respect, work, grades, and the type of friends I could have. I have basically the same policy, and my sons understand it.

As children get older and show good judgment, they naturally should be given more liberty to make their own decisions concerning an increasing number of things, including friendships. Yet we (Teresa and I) have monitored our kids' close friends and been involved in those choices, using several guidelines that I will pass along to you.

- *Understand the difference between your kids' acquaintances and those friends who are within their "spheres of influence."* Your child will gravitate toward certain kids for various reasons. These are the kids they "hang with." In other words, the kids they talk to on the phone, invite to the house, sit with in church, and so forth. Since you cannot monitor every peripheral relationship your child has, make sure you know who these friends are because these are the ones who will exercise influence over your kids.

- *As much as possible, make and take opportunities to get to know these friends personally.* Through the years, we have made arrangements for all three of our sons to have their friends over, whether to play, spend the night, or just "hang out." I find out all I can about them, asking questions about their church attendance, parents, and, if they are old enough, their relationship to Christ. I observe the way they talk, dress, show respect (or don't), and the way they play and interact with my family.

- *If my son is invited to a friend's house, I meet the parents, find out what activity might be planned outside of the home, and make sure there is going to be adequate supervision.* I assure the parents that my son will conduct himself as a Christian, and show courtesy and respect. I also ask that they inform me if there is a problem of any kind.

- *I watch for any signs that my child is indeed running with the wrong crowd.* These signs include:

  —A loss of interest in spiritual things.

  —An openly rebellious spirit.

  —An interest in music or dress that gravitates toward the distasteful or ungodly.

141

—The desire to attend functions or engage in activities that are questionable (such as certain movies, parties, etc.)

—Learning that one of their friends has either been in trouble on a constant basis or has an unsavory reputation. If I determine that a "friend" is really more of an enemy, I step in and cut the relationship off as much as possible.

Recently one of my sons had his eyes opened to a relationship he had been involved in with two girls at school. Through a distasteful experience that wound up involving our entire family, we discovered just how unsavory the character of these girls was. I immediately stipulated that he was not to have any further contact of any kind with these girls. The next day, while going to school, he looked at his mom and said, "I know you and Dad are right. I knew these girls were having a bad influence on me, and I needed Dad to 'lay down the law.'"

- *As my kids have gotten older, I have given them three basic principles to use in making sure their crowd is the right crowd:*

    —Find out if a potential friend has ever received Christ and lives a dedicated life for Him.
    —Purpose that those who reject Christ must also reject you.
    —Set certain standards of conduct, and when asked to compromise them, explain your relationship to Christ, your standard of conduct, and make the other person choose your friendship or the questionable activity.

3. KEEP A FRIEND

Once you do find a friend, guard that relationship as you would the gold at Fort Knox. I believe there are two "super glue" qualities that can permanently cement any friendship: *honesty* and *loyalty*.

Proverbs 27:6 reminds us, "Faithful are the wounds of a friend, but the kisses of an enemy are deceitful." A real friend may "wound" you by telling you the truth, but he will tell you the truth nonetheless. A real friend may not always tell you what you want to hear, but he will always tell you what you need to hear. In the short run it may hurt you, but in the long run it will help you.

If you would like to measure a relationship to determine whether it qualifies as a genuine friendship, here are two questions to ask of the other person:

- Can I trust him enough to be totally honest with me?

- Can I trust him enough to be totally honest with him?

Only a true friendship expects, and can survive, mutual honesty.

The other quality involved in keeping a friend is *loyalty*. Solomon said, "There is a friend who sticks closer than a brother" (Prov. 18:24). The word *stick* refers to how the skin sticks to the bone. It is a poignant picture of just how close-knit one friend should be to another. Loyalty is one thing a person should never have to question about his friend. A true friend will always be your defense attorney before he becomes your judge.

There is no such thing as a "fair weather friend." You don't need friends in fair weather; you need them when it gets nasty! A fair weather friend is truly no friend at all.

I've read several definitions of a friend. The late Erma Bombeck said, "A friend is somebody who won't go on a diet when you're fat." Someone else said, "A friend is someone who multiplies your joys and divides your grief." But the best definition I have ever read is this one: "A friend is someone who will walk into your house when the whole world has just walked out."

On one occasion I had the privilege of meeting a tremendous Christian by the name of Charles Colson. Colson was known as President Richard Nixon's "hatchet man" before Watergate and spent some time in prison for his part in the cover-up. Through the trauma of his experiences, Colson became a Christian and later wrote the best-seller *Born Again*. In the book he told how he was invited to speak at a western university soon after his release from prison. There was still much hostility toward the entire Watergate crowd, especially Richard Nixon.

Questions were being thrown at him rapid fire and the students were becoming increasingly hostile. One student stood up and referred to a vicious criticism that Henry Kissinger had leveled at Richard Nixon. "Mr. Colson," he demanded, "do you agree with this criticism?" Colson said he scanned the room and could tell every ear was listening to hear what he would say. Here's how he replied: "We all know Mr. Nixon's negative qualities. He has been dissected in the press like no one in history. I could tell you his good points, but I don't believe I could persuade you to accept them. But what it comes down to is, no, I don't go along with Henry Kissinger's comments. Mr. Nixon is my friend, and I don't turn my back on my friends."[7]

Colson said for a moment he thought the roof would fall in—and in a way, it did; but not as he expected. There was a moment of silence, followed by a thunderous, standing ovation. The reason? Even hostile students could appreciate loyalty to a friend.

If you ever want to find out who your friends really are, just make a mistake! Many of those who you thought were your friends will desert you like rats on a sinking ship. So Solomon admonished in Proverbs 27:10, "Do not forsake your own friend or your father's friend."

BE COMPASSIONATE WITH FOES

In life, your children need to know that they will make foes as well as friends. It just comes with the territory. The issue is not, will they make enemies? The issue is, how will they respond to them? Friends can bring out the best in us, but, oh, how our foes can bring out the worst in us! Solomon passed two words of counsel along to his children concerning their foes.

1. FACE THEM WITH FORGIVENESS

Do not rejoice when your enemy falls,
And do not let your heart
    be glad when he stumbles;

Lest the LORD see it, and it displease Him,
And He turn away His wrath from him.
Do not fret because of evildoers,
Nor be envious of the wicked;
For there will be no prospect for the evil man;
The lamp of the wicked will be put out.
(Prov. 24:17–20)

Don't allow the cancer of bitterness to destroy you; it is better to take your medicine now than to agonize later. Therefore, *never wish ill on your enemy and leave revenge to God.*

God can handle your foes and punish them far better than you ever could. When you try to take matters into your own hands, you not only dam up God's anger, but you hold back His vengeance (vv. 17–18).

Revenge is God's business, not ours. Paul put the matter succinctly, yet firmly, when he said, "Beloved, do not avenge yourselves, but rather give place to wrath; for it is written, 'Vengeance is Mine, I will repay,' says the Lord" (Rom. 12:19).

2. KILL THEM WITH KINDNESS

It is not enough merely to leave your enemies alone. We must be proactive and demonstrate love to them. Solomon said in Proverbs 25:21–22,

If your enemy is hungry, give him bread to eat;
And if he is thirsty, give him water to drink;
For so you will heap coals of fire on his head,
And the LORD will reward you.

Is your enemy hungry? Then cook him a hot meal. Is your enemy thirsty? Then give him a glass of homemade, ice-cold lemonade. The result? You will "heap coals of fire on his head." What does this mean? Charles Swindoll explains:

In ancient days, homes were heated and meals were fixed on a small portable stove, somewhat like our outside barbecue grills. Frequently, a person would run low on hot coals and would need to replenish his supply. The container was commonly carried on the head. So, as the individual passed beneath second-story windows, thoughtful people who had extra hot coals in their possession would reach out of the window and place them in the container atop his head. Thanks to the thoughtful generosity of a few folks, he would arrive at the site with a pile of burning coals on his head, and a ready-made fire for cooking and keeping warm. "Heaping burning coals on someone's head" came to be a popular expression for a spontaneous and courteous act one person would voluntarily do for another.[8]

It has been well said that the best way to defeat your enemy is to make a friend of him. That can be done only with godly kindness. Dad, teach your children, and remember yourself, you are never more like Jesus than when you return good for evil and love your enemies.

Years ago there was a man in our church who got extremely angry with me over a situation I had to handle in the church not long after I came. He confronted me in an angry fashion after one service and then left. I thought he would not return but he did—angrier than ever. I was not in the wrong for what had transpired, but he was convinced that I was.

Each Sunday he would come to church, sit in one of the first couple of rows, fold his arms, and put on a face that said, "Bless me if you can." I dreaded seeing him come in each Sunday and even began to pray that he would stop coming. Then the Lord reminded me that there were two things this man could not fight: my prayers and my love.

I made a conscious effort to speak to him whenever he came in. I would force him to shake my hand. I would affirm his presence each time he attended, but nothing changed. I just kept praying for him and loving him as much as he would let me.

It took almost two years, but one day my secretary informed me that Mr. X had come to see me, if I would see him. I asked her to escort him into my office. I knew something was radically different when he said, "Hello, *Pastor*." Understand, in two years he had never called me anything (at least that I had heard).

No sooner had the door shut than he began to weep and said, "Pastor, I was wrong in the way I have treated you. I have come to ask for your forgiveness." I immediately embraced him and informed him that he had already been forgiven—and we have been good friends ever since. Quite frankly, it is still one of the highlights of my ministry.

I was reminded of Edwin Markham's beautiful poem:

He drew a circle that shut me out—
Heretic, rebel a thing to flout.
But love and I had the wit to win:
We drew a circle that took him in.[9]

BE CAUTIOUS WITH FOOLS

Three Hebrew words are used to describe the fool in Proverbs, all rendered by the same English word, *fool*. The Hebrew term *kesil* refers to the hardheaded person who thinks he needs no advice.

The term *'ewil* has a root meaning of "growing thick of fluids."[10] This refers to the thickheaded person who refuses to listen to counsel.

Finally, the Hebrew term *nabal* refers to the empty-headed person who carries out his lack of wisdom in a foolish lifestyle.[11]

The fool is an empty-headed, thickheaded, hardheaded, obstinate person who gets an *F* in the school of wisdom. The fool may be intellectually brilliant, financially successful, and socially admired, but he is morally and spiritually bankrupt. Solomon warned early on about the fool. In the very first chapter he said, "The fear of the

LORD is the beginning of knowledge, but fools despise wisdom and instruction" (Prov. 1:7).

Rather than list every verse in Proverbs dealing with the fool, I have noted the categories of people Proverbs marks as "fools." It would be a good exercise for dads to go over this list with their children to see if they know anyone who fits one of these categories. A fool is:

- The loud mouth who loves to hear himself talk, and forces others to do the same (18:2).

- The hot-tempered bully who thinks anger, violence, and the bigger gun proves his manhood (12:16; 14:16).

- The egotist who believes he is a "self-made man" and worships his "creator" (26:1).

- The person who lets praise swell his head rather than humble his heart (26:1).

- The pseudo-intellectual who thinks he knows more than God and ridicules the Bibl. (26:7, 9).

- The know-it-all who thinks he knows all there is to learn and what he doesn't know isn't worth learning (12:15a; 26:12). (The fool is often wrong, but never in doubt!)

- The rebellious child or teenager who loves evil, hates good, and thinks sin is a joke and righteousness is for sissies (10:23; 13:19; 14:9).

- The impulsive talker who *always* lets you know "what is on his mind" and is willing to give you "a piece of it" even when there is no piece to spare! (29:11)

- The ladder-climber who puts wealth, position, and material possessions above the happiness and well-being of his family (11:29).

- The divisive troublemaker who loves to start arguments, hates to stop them, and doesn't mind losing the war, as long as he wins the battle (20:3).

- The wasteful spendthrift who blows money faster than he earns it, saves nothing, and gives even less to God. He knows the price of everything and the value of nothing (21:20).

- The self-confident person who trusts his own heart, mind, and judgment, rather than the God who gave him all three (19:3; 28:25–26).

- The gossiping big mouth who spreads slander, lies, and half-truths, not caring who it hurts. Usually he has enough cowardice to talk about a person, but not enough courage to talk to a person (10:18).

- The hardheaded child or teenager who hates the wise instruction of a godly father and breaks the heart of a godly mother (10:1; 15:5).

- The stubborn sinner who never learns from his mistakes and keeps doing the same thing repeatedly while expecting different results (26:11).

One of the reasons Solomon wanted to instill wisdom in the hearts of his children was to keep them away from fools and so to keep them from becoming fools themselves. He did not want them to become fools, for "fools die for lack of wisdom" (Prov. 10:21). Just as the body will die for lack of oxygen, a man will ultimately and eternally die from a lack of wisdom.

It is the lack of wisdom that causes a "debased mind," which leads the homosexual, the adulterer, or the idolater into "exchanging the truth of God for the lie, retaining God in their knowledge," so that they "receive in themselves the penalty of their error which was due" (Rom. 1:25, 27–28).

How should your son or daughter relate to fools? By saturating his or her presence with their absence. "Go from the presence of a foolish man, when you do not perceive in him the lips of knowledge" (Prov. 14:7). The bottom line is this: Only a fool fools around with fools!

One of the most valuable lessons you can teach your children is how to evaluate potential friends. The following list of questions can help your children to determine who should be included in that special circle called friends—questions you should ask of their friends as well.

- *Does this person profess to know Christ as Savior and Lord?* (Prov. 12:26) (This does not necessarily mean that your children cannot associate with lost youth—but it does mean your child, and you, will give a concentrated and concerned effort to win them to Christ. However, make plain that Scripture *does* preclude dating a lost person.)

- *Does this person draw me closer to God or farther from Him?* (4:14–17)

- *Is this person actively involved in church?* (Heb. 10:24–25) (Again, this does not preclude a relationship if the child does not attend church, but it does open the door to include church as a part of a true friendship.)

- *What kind of other friendships does this person keep?* What kind of crowd does he run with? (Prov. 13:20)

- *Does he try to involve me in questionable or wrong activities?* (1:10–16)

- *Does he show respect to his own parents?* What kind of relationship does he have with his own family? (10:1; 15:5*)*

- *Does he control his tongue?* Does he use profanity, obscenities, or vulgarities in his speech? (10:32; 15:28)

- *Does he have a violent temper or does he exercise reasonable self-control?* (29:22)

- *Does he have a positive attitude or a negative one?* (16:28; 22:11)

- *Is he trustworthy and honest?* Can he be relied upon to be loyal and true? (18:24)

Dad, these are just a few questions you and your children might ask, not only about others to evaluate their friendships, but also about themselves to evaluate their own worth as a friend. Again, one cannot be too careful in choosing one's friends.

BECOME YOUR CHILD'S BEST FRIEND

One last question: What kind of friendship do you have with your own children? Dad, the best person to teach your child about relationships—and especially about friendship—is you. Why not show your children what a friend is by being their very best friend?

Taped to the bookshelf in my study (where I can see it from my desk every day) is a letter to me from my youngest son, Joshua. He wrote it in November of 1995, one month before his tenth birthday. I think you'll be able to see why I like to read it every day:

> I love you, Dad. I will never forget you. You are the greatest dad ever. Words can't express my thoughts about you. I love you more than anything. You are my very best friend. The whole time I was at school today I was thinking about you and wanting to be with you. At home when you prayed with me I had the greatest day ever.
>
> I love you,
> Joshua Merritt

That letter means far more to me than a letter from George Washington! Dad, when you get right down to it, *friendship is what fatherhood is all about*. You *can* be your child's best friend. Remember, one part of friendship is giving wise counsel, for as Solomon the father (and, I believe, his children's best friend) said, "The heartfelt counsel of a friend is as sweet as perfume and incense" (Prov. 27:9). So don't be shy in counseling your child about his relationships, even while keeping your relationship with him the most special of all!

PART 3

STANDING UP
IN A FALLING DOWN
WORLD

Chapter 10

HOW TO KEEP DENNIS FROM BECOMING A MENACE

The thing that impresses me most
about America, is the way parents
obey their children.

—Edward, Duke of Windsor (1894–1972)

I am well aware of the old saying, "Fools rush in where angels fear to tread."[1] Nevertheless, I am going to take the plunge and tackle a subject that is, at one and the same time, crucial and extremely controversial, but even more consequential: the rearing and discipline of children.

- It is *crucial* because we are seeing an unprecedented breakdown in civility and authority in our nation, caused largely by the breakdown of authority in the home.

- It is *controversial* because God's Word says one thing, while many educators, sociologists, and child psychologists are saying another.

- It is *consequential* because juvenile delinquency is increasing seven times faster than the population. Why the rapid increase? One primary reason: delinquent parents.

155

A newspaper article headlined, "Fortress-like Dallas School Points Way" is just a sign of the times:

> The public school of the future is open now—in Dallas.
>
> Townview Magnet Center, a $41 million state-of-the-art schoolhouse, opened this school year.
>
> With parents, politicians and school officials across the nation concerned about rising violence on school campuses, the Texas facility is likely to set the standard for new schools, particularly those in urban districts located in or near high-crime neighborhoods.
>
> It is a sprawling brick building with thirty-seven surveillance cameras, six metal detectors, five full-time police officers, and a high-tech environmental design geared toward crime prevention.
>
> That design features unusually wide halls, straight lines without nooks and crannies, lots of windows so that the school grounds can be viewed easily from inside, perimeter lights in all public spaces, and an iron pole fence that separates the school from the adjacent neighborhood.
>
> "We've decided to overdo it up-front to overpower this issue," Dallas School District Superintendent, Chad Woolery told the *New York Times*. "We want to make sure that safety is not an issue so kids can concentrate on learning." ... There is something sad about a school like Townview that is as much fortress as it is learning institution. But, given the realities of life in so many of our public schools today, it is hard to argue against it.[2]

What does all of this have to do with the discipline of children in the home? Simply everything. Former Commissioner of Education Ernest L. Boyer correctly sized up the situation when he said, "The schools are a reflection of the world around them. Schools don't operate in a vacuum. You show me a school that has discipline and high standards, and I'll find you homes in a community that operate along those value systems. A school that has become chaotic, and where there is a lack of respect and commitment to work hard, probably reflects behavior that occurs once children leave the school."[3]

THE POISON OF PERMISSIVENESS

There is a poison infiltrating our society today that is odorless, tasteless, soundless, and sightless. It is ruining children, ransacking character, and robbing cheer from our homes, schools, and churches. What is this deadly poison? It is the *poison of permissiveness*.

Chuck Swindoll has made a pungent observation concerning the rebellion and disobedience that seems to be running rampant among so many American young people today:

> Teachers see it in today's classrooms; merchants face it in their shops; cops encounter it on a daily basis; youth workers in churches across America are forever forced to deal with it. Why? BECAUSE PARENTS WON'T. The permissiveness found in homes today is downright disgusting. It is not uncommon to find child-centered homes where children intimidate their parents. Afraid to be strong, hesitant to stand firm against the determined will of their youngster, parents create a domestic setting that becomes unbearable.[4]

I admit up-front that what I am going to say is naturally colored by the way I was reared as a child. Most of us have seen the timeless commercial where the distinguished gentleman looks into the camera and says, "We make money the old-fashioned way—we *earn* it." Well, I received my whippings as a child the old-fashioned way—I earned them! I freely admit (and now, gratefully; though not back then!) that I was reared in a home where firm, but godly, discipline was practiced. My dad could clear leather quicker than Wyatt Earp!

I know that I cannot be a "spoiled child," because my dad did not "spare the rod."

But here I want to speak as a dad to dads: Regardless of how you view the discipline of children, both in its necessity and in its application, the Scripture rightly says, "Sow the wind, and reap the whirlwind" (Hos. 8:7). As Leonardo da Vinci once put it, "He who does not punish evil, commands it to be done."

HOW TO RUIN YOUR KIDS

Years ago, the United States Chamber of Commerce published an article with a list of twelve rules on "How to Train Your Child to Be a Delinquent." Dad, you would do well to take a moment and read these, carefully and thoughtfully:

1. When your kid is still an infant, give him everything he wants. This way he will think the world owes him a living when he grows up.

2. When he picks up swearing and off-colored jokes, laugh at him, encourage him. As he grows up he will pick up cuter phrases that will floor you.

3. Never give him any spiritual training. Wait until he is twenty-one and let him decide for himself.

4. Avoid using the word *wrong*. It will give your child a guilt complex. You can condition him to believe later, when he is arrested for stealing a car, that society is against him and he is being persecuted.

5. Pick up after him—his books, shoes, and clothes. Do everything for him so he will be experienced in throwing all responsibility onto others.

6. Let him read all printed material he can get his hands on—[never think of monitoring his TV programs]. Sterilize the silverware, but let him feast his mind on garbage.

7. Quarrel frequently in his presence, and then he won't be too surprised when his home is broken up later.

8. Satisfy his every craving for food, drink, and comfort. Every sensual desire must be gratified; denial may lead to harmful frustrations.

9. Give your child all the spending money he wants. Don't make him earn his own. Why should he have things as tough as you did?

10. Take his side against neighbors, teachers, and policemen; they're all against him.

11. When he gets into real trouble, make up excuses for yourself by saying, "I never could do anything with him; he's just a bad seed."

12. Prepare for a life of grief.[5]

The preceding formula is a surefire recipe for making Dennis a Menace, but I have good news for all parents: Dennis may become a menace, but it doesn't have to be because of poor parenting.

For you dads who have thrown up your hands from time to time and screamed out, "Help, I'm a parent!" (believe me, if you haven't gotten there yet, you will), there is hope for the hopeless and help for the helpless. The Ultimate Father has given His infinitely wise philosophy on home building and child rearing, and it can be a life preserver to many families who are sinking in a sea of conflict, quarreling, and rebellion.

Before I plunge fully into this topic, let me remind you what John Wilmot, the Earl of Rochester, once said: "Before I got married I had six theories about bringing up children. Now I have six children and no theories." As a father of three sons with seventeen-plus years of "active duty" under my belt, I can relate to old John! This chapter will contain no theories—simply practical principles from Proverbs that are tried, tested, and proven in the laboratory of life.

LAYING THE FOUNDATION

A pithy little proverb nestled right in the middle of his book summarizes Solomon's counsel on this matter of rearing children: "Train up a child in the way he should go, and when he is old he will not depart from it" (Prov. 22:6).

Whether or not you have heard that verse before, you may find yourself muttering under your breath, "Is that it?" But before you dismiss this short statement as simplistic, consider that it contains an ocean of profound truth, able, if properly understood and applied, to make a world of difference in you as a parent and in your children.

In the 1992 presidential campaign, Bill Clinton's manager, James Carville, encapsulated the driving concern of the election with four simple words: "It's the economy, stupid!"

Well, I would like to ask all dads to remember one thing: When it comes to the discipline, training, and rearing of your children: "It's the timing, dads!"

The subject of Proverbs 22:6 is a child. The word *train* can be translated "dedicate." In other words, it is from childbirth that we are to dedicate our children to the Lord, and the instruction of discipline is to start when children are young. There may be a dad reading this chapter who needs to stop worrying about what Junior will do when he grows up, put this book down, and go see what he's up to *now!*

Solomon is not advising us on how to train up a teenager or a young man; his advice is on how to "train up a *child*." There are several reasons why it is important to start early in the training and disciplining of children.

First, *the will is more flexible.* A twig is much easier to bend than a trunk. The time to train a child in the ways of life and teach a child the things of God, is when that child is young. In the early years, the child's will is like soft clay, malleable and pliable. In other words, it is when they are young that you are to "set their ways," for when they get older their "ways are set."

The Hebrew phrase "train up" came from agrarian terminology, which referred to training a tree or vine to grow in a particular shape or direction.[6] If you have ever been to Disney World, you have seen those fascinating shrubs shaped like animals and various Disney characters. Recently, I had the privilege of going backstage at Disney World, and I saw how those bushes were formed.

Of course, those bushes don't grow that way by themselves! (Even Disney doesn't have that kind of magic.) Over a ten- to fifteen-year period, from the time those bushes are planted, they are shaped, trimmed, pruned, and "trained" in the way that they should go. Some parts are removed, other parts are cultivated, and still other parts are trimmed away; finally, the entire plant conforms to a wire mesh in the shape of the desired animal or character.

That is exactly the process by which we are to train our children. It must begin early. To put it another way: "If you wait till they date, it's too late!" Solomon gave this reminder: "Chasten your son *while there is hope*, and do not set your heart on his destruction" (Prov. 19:18). I can't tell you how many times parents in my church have come to my office, brokenhearted over their children, and saying something like this: "My kids are hopeless." The vast majority of the time when I do a little investigation, I find the reason why their kids are hopeless: The parents didn't train their children while there was still hope.

You can almost hear the urgency in Solomon's voice as he said, "He who spares his rod hates his son, but he who loves him disciplines him *promptly* (Prov. 13:24). The Hebrew word for "promptly," *shakar,* originally meant "dawn, early in the day." It came to mean pursuing something early in life. Dad, the two greatest words of advice I can give you on rearing your children is: START EARLY.

You may have a little darling running around your house right now who you think is a little angel. But trust me, one day those legs will get longer, those wings will get shorter, and sometimes those little "angels" even sprout horns!

You don't have to be a rocket scientist to figure out that it is far easier to talk to and reason with a child in his younger years than when he becomes a teenager. Why? Simply because when they are young they are more apt and ready to listen to your advice and counsel. Children are hungry to learn, and they haven't yet reached the age where they think they know everything and you know nothing.

Mark Twain said that when he was fourteen years old he thought his father was the dumbest man in the world. By the time he reached twenty-one, he was amazed how much his dad had learned in seven years! That attitude is becoming ever more typical of adolescents. So, dad, teach your children while they will listen to you because the day will come when they won't.

Incidentally, while they are in the listening stage, you should be in the talking, teaching stage. Take the opportunity to read the Bible to your children. Use everyday experiences to teach them what God's Word has to say about the Golden Rule, how to be polite, how to forgive, and how to confess and repent of sin. Never underestimate God's ability to develop spiritual character and to teach spiritual truths to your children even at a very early age.

TENDER IS THE YOUNG HEART

Still another reason to start early is because when children are young, *the heart is more tender.* I will never give you a better piece of advice in this book than this one: Make sure that you lead your children to Christ personally and as early as possible. I believe in legitimate child evangelism, and I'm convinced that, by and large, the parents ought to be the evangelists. I understand we must be careful and make sure that our children understand basic truths about sin and salvation, but I know children can come to know Christ at an early age if raised in a proper, spiritual atmosphere.

Do you realize that some of the greatest Christians who ever lived were saved at an early age? For example:

- Jonathan Edwards was saved at the age of eight.

- Charles Spurgeon was saved at the age of twelve.

- Matthew Henry, the great commentator, was saved at the age of eleven.

- Polycarp, the courageous early church martyr, was saved at the age of nine.

162

- Ninety percent of all Southern Baptist missionaries were saved before the age of eleven, and the average age of conversion is eight.

There is a story about a woman who came to her pastor and said, "Pastor, how early should I start the serious spiritual training of my child?" The pastor asked, "How old is the child?" She answered, "Five." He replied, "Lady, you are five years too late." That pastor could not have been more right.

Andre Agassi is simply wrong when he says, "Image is everything." When it comes to the rearing of children, a more accurate statement can't be made than "Timing is everything." So, parents, don't delay. The longer you wait, the harder it gets.

BACK TO BASICS

As I have scoured through Proverbs, trying to get into the mind and heart of a dad who faced the same problems with his children that we do with ours, I found four basic principles that I believe will be helpful and will guide all of us who are seeking to be not only good parents, but godly parents. Following these principles will help us to become the best parents that we can be. Let me say as I list these principles that not only do they concern qualities that you should desire to give to your children, but, just as important, they are qualities that your children deserve from you.

1. THE PRINCIPLE OF AFFECTION

One statement of Solomon's bears repeating: "He who spares his rod hates his son, but he who loves him disciplines him promptly" (Prov. 13:24). If there is a dad reading this chapter who is afraid that discipline will drive his child from him, Solomon said just the opposite is true. Rather than causing your child to question your love, discipline affirms and confirms your love. Love and discipline go together. If you love a child, you will discipline the child; and you will discipline the child in love.

I do not buy the age-old excuse that parents don't discipline their children because they "love them too much." The truth is, if you don't discipline your child, it's not because you love him too much; it is because you love *you* too much! I am not surprised that a 1980 Gallup poll revealed that more than 90 percent of graduating high school seniors wished their parents and teachers loved them enough to discipline them more and require more of them.[7]

As you know, water follows the path of least resistance. I know it is much easier to let things slide, avoid confrontation, stick your head in the sand, and hope things will get better than it is to suffer the pain of disciplining one of your children. Keep in mind, however, that the only person who ever got anywhere by letting something slide was a trombone player.

There was a method to Solomon's madness when he wrote,

> My son, do not despise the
>   chastening of the LORD,
> Nor detest His correction;
> For whom the LORD loves He corrects,
> Just as a father the son in whom he delights.
>   (Prov. 3:11–12)

Just let that sink in. The greatest and wisest father of all is God. God not only loves, God *is* love. Yet we read here that a loving God is a God who disciplines. So try this on for an earth-shattering thought: *Any parents who refuse to discipline their children are really saying that they are better parents than God.*

Remember, love always does what is best for the other person. Discipline is painful, oftentimes distasteful, and sometimes downright depressing, but there are times that love demands and commands discipline and training for the child.

2. THE PRINCIPLE OF DIRECTION

Listen closely to this proverb: "Foolishness is bound up in the heart of a child; the rod of correction will drive it far from him" (Prov. 22:15; for the meaning of "beat" and "rod," see rule 3 under "Five Rules for Effective Discipline" below). Notice here that the concern is with foolishness, not folly nor fun. You are not to discipline a child just because he acts like a child (how else can he act?). You should not discipline a child because he makes childlike mistakes, like knocking his milk over or (even more infuriating) laughing at his sister when *she* knocks *her* milk over.

"Foolishness" may sound mischievous to us, but to the Hebrew way of thinking it was a far more serious matter. In Proverbs, the opposite of foolishness is wisdom, and the lack of wisdom results in wickedness. Foolishness here equates to wickedness. Foolishness is the spirit of rebellion that despises discipline and disrespects authority.

The natural tendency of any child is to rebel (this has been true since the garden of Eden). This tendency must be "driven" from the child. Just as a car, out of line, tends to drift and needs constant correction, every child is born spiritually "out of line" and needs to be constantly corrected by his parents.

That is why Solomon went on to observe, "The rod and rebuke give wisdom, but a child left to himself brings shame to his mother" (Prov. 29:15). Now, why is this true? It is true because a child left to himself is a child left in the condition in which he was born. He was born "out of line." He was born "in foolishness." The child must, therefore, learn moral authority. He must learn that for every action there is a reaction.

Dad, you would be wise to remember that you are a tool in the hands of God to direct a child from where he *would* go to where he *should* go. This is the purpose as well as the necessity of godly discipline, which is to be given via "the rod of correction."

3. THE PRINCIPLE OF CORRECTION

Too many parents make the mistake of always telling a child when he is wrong, rather than also taking the time to tell a child how to get right, be right, and stay right. Biblical correction involves both. The number one extrabiblical beatitude for all parents is, "Blessed are the balanced."

Solomon went on to write, "Correct your son, and he will give you rest; yes, he will give delight to your soul" (Prov. 29:17). The word *correct* means to chastise, to reprove, or to force back to the right way. Always remember that discipline is like a two-edged sword; it is not only to correct children when they are wrong, but to direct them to a way that is right.

All of this leads me to make one of the strongest statements in this chapter. Dad, *you may as well quit trying to win a popularity contest with your children.* Your children are not always going to like you. But if you will discipline them, correct them, keep them from going the wrong way, and continually force them back to the right way, they will love you—and eventually they will grow to like you again.

4. THE PRINCIPLE OF PROTECTION

It may never have occurred to you as a parent that discipline is a form of protection, but this idea comes straight from Solomon himself:

> Do not withhold correction from a child,
> For if you beat him with a rod,
>   he will not die.
> You shall beat him with a rod,
> And deliver his soul from hell.
>   (Prov. 23:13–14)

Now we see what truly is at stake in this matter of disciplining children. May I be frank with you? My primary concern is not your happiness or your peace of mind; it is the very soul of your child. Discipline, or the lack thereof, can set off a positive or a negative chain reaction.

If a child will not respect authority in the home, he will not respect it in the school, the government, the church, or, ultimately, even heaven itself. It is just a small step from rebelling against the parents that God gave a child to rebelling against the God who gave the child his parents.

FIVE RULES FOR EFFECTIVE DISCIPLINE

With these thoughts in mind, let me suggest five rules to follow rigidly in the area of discipline.

1. DISCIPLINE SHOULD BEGIN EARLIER THAN LATER

When a child is old enough to disobey willingly and knowingly; when a child is old enough to know right from wrong and chooses wrong over right; when a child is old enough to be told to do what is right and then does what is wrong anyway—that child is ready to be disciplined.

By the way, don't impose too limited an age limit on this definition of "child." Just because your child is old enough to drive, shave, or date, doesn't mean he or she is beyond your correction and your discipline. Certainly children reach an age where spanking is inappropriate; but even though your child may be too old for corporal punishment, there are other (and more effective ways) to discipline an adolescent or a teenager. If you read Proverbs carefully enough, you will find that Solomon was talking to a son who was old enough to join a street gang, be tempted by sexual sin, patronize prostitutes, get into debt, and drink. He was not talking only about first graders.

Whether you are a father or the head of your household, glue this to your heart: *As long as your children are under your roof, they are under your authority.* You will give an account to God for the authority that you exercised over your children.

2. MAKE SURE THE GUIDELINES ARE CLEAR

Child psychologists discovered an interesting truth several years ago. Contemporary thought assumed that fences on playgrounds made children feel restricted in their recreation. Based on that belief, it was decided to remove the fences so children would not feel confined. To the astonishment of the experts, the opposite effect occurred. Researchers found that the children became more inhibited with their activities. They tended to huddle toward the middle of the playground and exhibited signs of insecurity. When the fences were replaced, the children once more played with greater enthusiasm and freedom.

The lesson? We all need boundaries—something to define the limits of safety and security. The "experts" suggested that boundaries restrict creativity, but as the children on the playground demonstrated, we need a clear understanding of what is safe and acceptable so that our creativity can flourish.[8] Children will flourish, and you will function better as a dad if guidelines are clearly communicated and the consequence of not following those guidelines completely understood. Let me give you a practical example.

I recently had the joy (?) of buying my first son, James Jr., an automobile. Before I gave him the keys to the car, he signed a contract that I drew up. We went over every item of that contract and then we both signed it. Here is the contract we signed:

CONTRACT WITH CHARACTER FOR A CAR

1. I agree to pay for all of the gas.

2. I will pay part of the insurance, portion mutually agreed upon by me and my parents.

3. Any speeding violations will result in loss of driving privileges of up to one month, depending on the severity of the violation.

4. I understand there will be a graduated schedule of where I can travel and will increase with experience, age, and demonstrated maturity.

5. If I incur any accidents that are my fault, I will lose one month of driving privileges.

6. Only passengers approved by both sets of parents may be transported and then only one passenger at a time without special permission by Mom and Dad.

7. Reckless driving will incur loss of driving privileges of up to one month.

8. Any grade below a B will result in the loss of driving privileges of one month.

9. No parking in secluded spots with a member of the opposite sex *under any circumstances.*

10. On school nights I will be allowed one night a week out with curfew at 8:00 P.M. unless special permission is granted.

11. Whereabouts must be given to Mom and Dad at all times within reason.

12. One night out per weekend: Fri. P.M. curfew 11:30, Sat. P.M. curfew 10:30 (exceptions to curfews granted per individual case/circumstances).

13. Chores must be done at home as part of maintaining driving privileges.

14. Attitude, obedience, responsibility, and conduct may determine availability of car.

15. I may only take either brother when prior permission is granted or in case of an emergency.

I, the undersigned, understand and agree to adhere to all of the conditions of the above and fix my signature thereto.

Signature:_____ (Driver)

Signature:_____ (Parents)

Before he ever turned the ignition switch, my son clearly understood the guidelines under which he could keep the privilege of driving the car. There is a humorous story of a father who gave his sixteen-year-old son his first car. Before he handed the lad the keys he said, "This is a magic car." "Really?" the boy replied. "Yeah," answered the dad. "One speeding ticket, and it will disappear." Every parent might think of giving their kids a "magic" car.

3. DISCIPLINE SHOULD BE APPROPRIATELY RENDERED

Repeatedly in Proverbs, Solomon refers to the "rod" (10:13; 13:24; 22:15; 23:13–14; 26:3; 29:15). The term translated "rod" is used in the Old Testament for the scepter of a king or the staff of a shepherd. In other words, dad, you are not a dictator. The rod is to enable you to rule your family righteously, like a good king, and to lead your children lovingly like a good shepherd. The rod is a God-given tool of discipline.

Incidentally, the rod is to be used to "smite" the child, not to "beat" the child. The Hebrew term for "beat," *naw-kaw,* is used, for example, for the smiting of an object with one nonfatal strike, such as a donkey (Num. 22:23). The root word even refers to the smiting of the conscience (1 Sam. 24:5).[9] The point is that Solomon was advocating neither child abuse nor literal beatings. He did advocate corporal punishment that sufficiently smites the child's conscience, brings him to repentance, and sets him back on the good path of wisdom.

In other words, when your children are younger, you should not only be on speaking terms with them, but you should be on spanking terms with them.

I believe in corporal punishment because the Bible teaches it and God approves it. However, let me give these caveats. On the one hand, spankings usually need to be few and far between. You will find that when you give a good spanking, and make it stick, you won't have to spank your child very often.

Billy Graham described the time his two-year-old son spit at him in a fit of anger. Mr. Graham said, "I don't know where he learned such an ugly habit, but one thing I know for certain. If that boy chews tobacco when he grows up, he'll swallow the juice because after what I did to him, he will never spit again."[10]

On the other hand, as I have already said, no child should ever be abused, tortured, beaten, struck with a hand or fist, slapped in the face, or disciplined in a fit of anger. That's not discipline; that's abuse, and the Bible roundly condemns it.

4. WHEN YOUR CHILDREN ARE YOUNG, YOU AIM HIGH WHEN YOU AIM LOW!

Solomon sagely stated, "Wisdom is found on the lips of him who has understanding, but a rod is for the back of him who is devoid of understanding" (Prov. 10:13). It is interesting that the Hebrew word for "back" is *gar*, which literally means "in the middle of the back," i.e., the backside of the anatomy.[11] If you take a tape measure and measure a child from top to bottom, you will find that the middle of the back is just about where they sit down! (Could that be God's divine location for an old-fashioned hickory stick?)

5. DISCIPLINE IS TO BE GIVEN PRIVATELY

The purpose of discipline is instruction not humiliation. You are never to embarrass a child in public, and never discipline a child in anger.

I know that some parents believe in talking to children and never spanking them. Perhaps that works for you. Just be careful that your child does not wind up like one little boy I heard of. He was visiting his grandmother, and they talked about many things until the topic of discipline came up.

"Does your father have to spank you very often?" asked the grandmother.

"Oh no, my daddy never has spanked me," answered the little boy.

"He doesn't? What does he do?" wondered the grandmother.

"He just talks to me when I misbehave," replied the boy.

"What does he say?" the grandmother asked.

"I don't know," the boy said. "I never listen."

Let me caution that spanking should always be the last resort, not the first resource. Proverbs 29:15 gives us the perfect balance: "The *rod* and *reproof* give wisdom." The rod (corporeal punishment) and reproof (verbal correction) give wisdom. Reproof should almost always be used before, and without, the rod; oftentimes it can make the rod unnecessary. But when reproof is not enough, let the rod come to the rescue!

HELPING THE BOY TO SIT DOWN AND THE MAN TO STAND UP

We dads must never lose sight of an overriding purpose of discipline, which is the "training up" of our children. I want to digress for only a moment by returning to Proverbs 22:6 to investigate the term "train up." In Hebrew, that phrase roots back to a term referring to the palate or the roof of the mouth.

In Bible days, a Hebrew mother would wean her baby off of milk by taking her index finger and dipping it into a tiny pool of crushed grapes or dates. She would then place that finger into the mouth of the child and massage the gums, the palate, and the roof of the mouth, thereby creating a sucking response. This would soon cultivate a hungry sensation within the baby's mouth, along with a desire for more food. In this way the child was taught to crave, and then swallow, solid food.

Solomon is giving us here a gentle reminder that we are not to ram truth down the throats of our children, but are to make them hungry for it so they will freely swallow it and digest it. It should go without saying, Dad, that the best way to get your children to accept the truth is not just to teach it, but to live it.

We are then told to train up a child "in the way he should go." The word *way* is extremely picturesque. It refers to the bending of a bow. Literally it says, "Train up a child in his way." That is, train up a child in the way he is "bent." Walter Kaiser explained the concept perfectly:

> What is the "way"? It could mean the way that the child ought to go according to God's law: the proper way in light of God's revelation. It could also mean the way best fitting the child's own personality and particular traits.
>
> Which is correct? There is no doubt that the first presents the highest standard and more traditional meaning. However, it has the least support from the Hebrew idiom and seems to be a cryptic way to state what other proverbial expressions would have done much more explicitly.
>
> Therefore, we conclude that this enigmatic phrase means that instruction ought to be conformed to the nature of the youth. It ought to regulate itself according to the stage of life, evidence of God's unique calling of the child, and the manner of life for which God is singling out that child.[12]

Put simply, every child is to be trained in the way of the Lord, but in the words of Derek Kidner, in "respect for his individuality and vocation, though not his selfwill."[13] The *Amplified Bible* captures the sense perfectly: "Train up a child in the way he should go [*and in keeping with his individual gift or bent*], and when he is old he will not depart from it."[14]

In other words, the verse is not only referring to the material of instruction (the wisdom found in God's Word), but also to the *manner* of instruction that is to be governed by the child's unique stage of life, personality, and giftedness—in other words, his personal bent.[15]

This cannot be stressed enough. Your children are just like my three sons—all different from one another. I have had to learn that I cannot treat every child exactly the same way. Of course, certain principles apply to all of our children, but you cannot always treat children in the same way for the simple reason that all children are not the same.

Therefore, let me give you two mistakes to avoid at all cost:

1. *Don't try to make your children into what you used to be.* Just because you were a football player doesn't mean your son will want to be one. Just because you made straight A's in school, doesn't mean your children are capable of a 4.0 grade point average. I am not trying to excuse laziness, but not every child is equally gifted athletically or intellectually.

2. *Don't try to make them into what you wanted to be.* Don't try to live your life through your children. Just because you didn't become a professional football player doesn't mean you should try to force your son to become one. The verse says to train up a child in the way *he should go*, not the way you would go or the way you would want him to go.

There are three things we dads need to teach our kids continuously. We need to teach them to *know* who they are, *like* who they are, and *be* who they are. Indeed, those are the three marks of healthy self-esteem.

Finally, we are told, "and when he is old, he will not depart from it." Now, the word *old* does not refer so much to being an elderly man, as it refers to any age beyond that of a young child. That is, if you begin early with a child, continue right up through adolescence, the teenage years, and beyond—and train that child in godly principles according to his unique nature, setting a godly example before him—then, generally speaking, he will not depart from it.

Again, as Kaiser put it: "The *from it* refers to the training of youth which was conformed to God's work in the child's very nature and being."[16]

SOME APPLES DO FALL FAR FROM THE TREE

Right here I need to say a word to some dads who have read this chapter under a cloud of guilt. You have a prodigal child, and you wonder if you are a failure. I must remind you that there are exceptions to every rule. Remember, the Proverbs are not so much promises as they are principles and precepts.[17]

For example, sometimes we are told a child will not listen to the counsel of his parents. I am sure Solomon was giving a word of personal testimony when he wrote this: "A wise son heeds his father's instruction, but a scoffer does not listen to rebuke" (Prov. 13:1). Bad parents sometimes turn out good children, and good parents sometimes have bad children. Remember, God's first two children were put in a perfect paradise . . . and they rebelled anyway.

I am sure most of you dads have done your very best in trying to rear your children to love and fear God—and yet somehow they have gotten off the beaten path. They have rebelled against the Lord. Now, whether they will ever come back to the Lord, I cannot definitively say. I do know, however, that *there comes a time when the boy has to sit down and the man has to stand up.* That is, there comes a time when the child is no longer a child and has to take responsibility for his own actions. If you have done your best as a parent, don't let the devil unnecessarily put you on a guilt trip for something you cannot help.

174

Dad, don't take my word for it. Take God's Word for it, for His Word is true and His way is tested. Discipline normally pays rich dividends that will last for all eternity, but lack of discipline can cause rivers of tears to flow for unending generations.

A great illustration of this comes from two families, one named Edwards, the other named Jukes. They started out with differing philosophies and ended up with differing legacies—and the difference was discipline.

> The father of Jonathan Edwards was a minister. His mother was the daughter of a clergyman. Among their descendants were fourteen presidents of colleges, more than one hundred college professors, more than one hundred lawyers, thirty judges, sixty physicians, more than a hundred clergymen, missionaries, and theology professors, and about sixty authors. There is scarcely any great American industry that has not had one of his family among its chief promoters. Such is the product of one American Christian family, reared under the most favorable conditions.
>
> The contrast is presented in the Jukes family, which could not be made to study, would not work, and is said to have cost the State of New York a million dollars. Their entire record is one of pauperism and crime, insanity, and imbecility. Among their twelve hundred known descendants, three hundred and ten were professional paupers, four hundred and forty were physically wrecked by their own wickedness, sixty were habitual thieves, one hundred and thirty were convicted criminals, fifty-five were victims of impurity. Only twenty learned a trade (and ten of these learned in the state prison), and this notorious family produced seven murderers.[18]

Yes, discipline does make a difference! If Dennis becomes a Menace, he can poison a stream that pollutes a river that ruins an ocean. But if he is reared by godly principles, he can multiply his good influence and the influence of an entire family for generations to come.

WILL YOU CHOOSE TO STAY A FATHER?

I want to encourage you, Dad, to heed the wise advice of Paul Harvey in a magnificent piece titled, "I am going to stay a Father." A few may find it dogmatic; personally, I find it dynamic:

> At a time when being a buddy to one's son is popular, I am going to stay a father. I believe it may yet prove to have been a bit sad psychology when dads are called "Jim, Pete, Art, Tom or Jack" by their children. When Spock, Freud, Dewey, and Williams James have conspired to make Dad a minor stockholder on the home's board of directors, when women's rights, civil rights, people's rights, children's rights, and property rights have made it wrong for fathers to speak with authority, I am going to stay a father.
>
> If a gap exists between my sons and daughters, and myself, I am going to work hard to understand, but I am also going to work hard to be understood. . . .
>
> When they tell it like it is, I will listen, even if I like it better like it was. If old-fashioned things as prayer, Bible study, worship and faith in God ever seem to my children to be out of it, square, or whatever—I trust God's help to have faith enough to yet pray for them, and I pledge with Job to offer additional sacrifices for them.
>
> With love in our home, I will answer their questions about the facts of life, but at nudeness and lewdness I refuse to wink. Drinking and smoking are as out of place and unwanted in my home as profan-

ity or the plague; and if experimentation with drugs or marijuana is ever a problem, it will be in violation of my every prayer and request. No laissez faire attitude will be accepted here—even if the weed is legalized and "social-tripping" becomes as acceptable as social drinking.

I want my children to know that I make mistakes, that I am foolish, proud and often inconsistent. But I will not tolerate that as an excuse for my hypocrisy. I ask them to help me change as children should, and to expect me to help them change in the methods expected of a parent. Others may look to the under thirty crowd for the wisdom to throw away the past, and to say what will remain for future generations; others may let the off-spring in the house determine the foods, the music, and the spending of the household, but I am going to stay a father.[19]

Dads, we have a tough job, no doubt about it, but let us covenant together to stay the course and stay fathers. With the help of God's power, the wisdom of His Word, and the leadership of His Spirit, we can prayerfully keep Dennis from becoming a menace—and in the process, even help him become a disciple.

Chapter 11

HOW TO MINE YOUR OWN GOLD

The child is the father of the man.

—William Wordsworth (1770–1850)

I am by no means a connoisseur of country music. Frankly, for the most part, it doesn't appeal to my musical tastes. I do, however, get great amusement out of seeing some of the titles of country songs. I recently compiled a list of actual country music song titles that are absolutely classic. Incidentally, as Rush Limbaugh would say, "Folks, I'm not making this up."

- "If the Phone Doesn't Ring, It's Me"

- "It Must Be Your Baby, He's Too Ugly to Be Mine"

- "I've Enjoyed as Much of This as I Can Stand"

- "You're the Reason Our Kids are Ugly"

- "I Wouldn't Take Her to a Dogfight Even If I Thought She Could Win"

- "Don't Cry Down My Back Baby, You Might Rust My Spurs"

I don't sing them, nor do I listen to them; I just list them! But let me give you probably the all-time notorious country song title that most everybody will recognize: "She Got the Gold Mine, I Got the Shaft."

179

If this chapter were a country song, I would title it "God's Got the Gold Mine—Don't Get the Shaft." I want to return to Proverbs 2 and recall that Solomon compared wisdom to silver taken from a mine and to hidden treasures: "If you seek her [wisdom] as silver, and search for her as for hidden treasures" (Prov. 2:4).

In essence, this book contains nuggets of wisdom I have quarried with my own shovel from the mine shaft of God's Word. I have tried not only to share with my fellow dads eternal truths that can be practically applied in the life of their children, but also destroy some myths that have been perpetrated in our society concerning the rearing of our children.

I have tried to motivate the readers of this book to be proactive in encouraging the development of honesty, reliability, respect, godliness, and self-control in the lives of their children. Sadly, there are far too many dads today who, for one reason or another, have abdicated this responsibility.

In his magnificent book, *Why Johnny Can't Tell Right from Wrong,* William Kilpatrick says that part of the reason for this negligence lies in the influence of powerful myths (some old, some new) that dominate our thinking about child rearing. He identified these myths:

> *The myth of the "good bad boy."* American literature and film loves to portray "bad" boys as essentially lovable and happy. Tom Sawyer and Buster Brown are examples from the past; the various lovable brats featured in film and television are contemporary examples. This strand in the American tradition has such a powerful hold on the imagination that the word "obedience" is very nearly a dirty word in the American vocabulary. The myth of the "good bad boy" is connected to . . .
>
> *The myth of natural goodness.* This is the . . . idea that virtue will take care of itself if children are just allowed to grow in their own way.
>
> *The myth of expert knowledge.* In recent decades parents have deferred to professional authority in the matter of raising their children.

Unfortunately, the vast majority of child-rearing experts subscribe to the myth of natural goodness mentioned above. So much emphasis has been placed on the unique creative and spontaneous nature of children, that parents have come to feel that child rearing means adjusting themselves to their children, rather than having children learn to adjust to the requirements of family life.

The myth that moral problems are psychological. This myth is connected to all of the above. In this view, behavior problems are seen as problems in self-esteem, or as the result of unmet psychological needs. The old-fashioned idea that most behavior problems are the result of sheer "willfulness" on the part of children doesn't occur to the average child expert. If you look in the index of a typical child-rearing book, you will find that a great many pages are devoted to "self-esteem," but you are not likely to find the word "character" anywhere.

The myth that parents don't have the right to instill their values in their children. Once again the standard dogma here is that children must create their own values. But, of course, children have precious little chance to do that since the rest of the culture has no qualms about imposing values. Does it make sense for parents to remain neutral bystanders when everyone else—from script writers, to entertainers, to advertisers, to sex educators—insists on selling their values to children?[1]

I have written this book not only to answer a resounding no to the last question Mr. Kilpatrick raised, but also to give us fathers some divine ammunition as we go to war in fighting for the moral lives of our kids. I want, in this chapter, not only to make a "miner" out of every dad who will read this book, but also to enable you dads to make a "miner" out of the "minors" running around your house. Not only should you be able to give them the golden nuggets of wisdom that come from God's treasure chest, but you ought to be able to teach them how to mine gold for themselves. Your kids don't have to be in *Who's Who?* to know "What's What!"

Dad, you cannot communicate God's wisdom to your children until God has communicated His wisdom to you. Wisdom does not come gift-wrapped and laid at the foot of your bed each day. Like silver, it must be mined, excavated, and dug out from the mine shaft of God's Word. So roll up your sleeves, get on your hard hat, take a lantern and shovel, and let's go mining!

GOD LOVES PROSPECTORS

Think about it: Every time a miner discovers silver or gold, or someone discovers hidden treasure, it didn't "just happen." Two things are true for any miner or treasure hunter who really wants to strike gold. First, he must be *looking for it.* In the same way, we are told concerning wisdom, "Seek her as silver" (Prov. 2:4a). The Hebrew word for seek, *baw-kash*, gives the idea of a person relentlessly searching for something, believing that it exists and expecting to find it.[2] Just walking into a mine and glancing around won't cut it. If you want to get the gold or the silver, you've got to be looking for it.

Ask any miner, and he will tell you that gold doesn't strike you—you strike gold! But you will never strike gold unless you first go searching for it. Jewels of wisdom and understanding are "not usually discovered by a casual observer or a chance passerby. They are excavated and enjoyed instead by the diligent, devoted, and determined."[3]

Now, to look for gold or silver in a mine, you have to enter the shaft. I know of no treasure mined from a shaft never entered. There's an old saying that "the devil is not afraid of a Bible that has dust on it." An unopened Bible is like a neglected gold mine—it may be rich with gold, but people never mind that it is never mined!

The analogy is simple: If you want to "mine" the silver of God's wisdom, you must enter the shaft. "Entering the shaft" is simply opening the Bible. It is sad to know that while 93 percent of Americans own a Bible, half never read it, including 23 percent of all born-again Christians. According to the Barna Research Group, only 18 percent of Christians read the Bible every day.[4]

Dad, I beg you to read your Bible every day and to encourage your children to do the same. Don't give the age-old excuse, "The reason why I don't read it is because I don't understand it." We are going to deal with that one momentarily. Also, don't bother with the one that goes, "I'm too busy." The fact is, *we all have time to do what we* really *want to do.*

I share the sentiments of former President Woodrow Wilson:

> I am sorry for men who do not read the Bible every day; I wonder why they deprive themselves of the strength and of the pleasure. It is one of the most singular books in the world, for every time you open it, some old text that you have read a score of times suddenly beams with a new meaning. There is no other book that I know of, of which this is true; there is no other book that yields its meaning so personally, that seems to fit itself so intimately to the very spirit that is seeking its guidance.[5]

May I repeat myself once more? God's got the gold mine—don't get the shaft!

The second characteristic of a miner is that not only must he be looking for gold, he also must be *digging for it*. Every miner must have three things to do his job: a hard hat, a light, and a shovel (or pick ax). Let's look at each of them.

1. THE HARD HAT OF COMMITMENT

If you are going to dig for the silver of God's wisdom, you can't do without the *hard hat of commitment*. You must be determined that every day you are going to get in the Word of God, so that the Word of God can get into you.

2. THE LIGHT OF THE HOLY SPIRIT

Dad, let me give you some wonderful news: The same *Holy Spirit* who reveals the wisdom of God's Word to men like Billy Graham, Chuck Swindoll, and John MacArthur, also wants to reveal that wisdom to you.

Years ago I heard about a man who loved to study the Bible. Every time he came to something he did not understand, his friend, Charlie, would pop into his mind. Charlie was a great Bible student; he just seemed to ooze with biblical wisdom. Whenever this man encountered a Bible question, he would go to Charlie and say, "Charlie, what does this verse mean? What is God trying to say here?" One day, as this man was reading his Bible, the Holy Spirit of God spoke to him and said, "Why don't you ask Me? I'm the one who teaches Charlie."

Every Christian has within him the Spirit of revelation. The Holy Spirit yearns to speak to you through the Word of God. A great prayer to say as you begin your "mining" is, "Open my eyes, that I may see wondrous things from Your law" (Ps. 119:18).

3. THE SHOVEL OF PRAYER

Every true "miner" needs the *shovel of prayer*. Bible study and prayer must go together. You should pray before you read the Bible that God will help you to understand it, and then you should pray after you read the Bible that God will help you to apply what He has told you. God is like a faraway lover. The Bible is His letter communicating to you; prayer is the telephone you pick up to talk to Him.

Dad, it's crucial that you maintain a consistent daily time of Bible study and prayer with God. You have not completed the training of your children until you have modeled for them a strong walk with God. That's the best way to motivate them toward the same.

Bill Nelson, a congressman from Florida, flew on a space shuttle mission aboard the *Columbia* just prior to the *Challenger* disaster. He wrote a book titled *Mission* describing his experience and explaining, among other things, how difficult it is to maintain a proper orbit in space.

There is no resistance in space, so an astronaut can literally turn that huge orbiter over by himself. To maintain a proper orbit, the on-board computers constantly make course and altitude corrections by firing small rockets which make minute adjustments. Larger jets burn to make major adjustments. These rockets are critical, for if they don't consistently fire at the right time, the space vehicle can veer from its orbit and either go tumbling into outer space or crashing into earth's atmosphere.[6]

In the same way, left to ourselves, our lives will tend to veer out of orbit into the outer space of lukewarmness and indifference or into the burning atmosphere of sin and downright rebellion. The twin rockets of prayer and Bible study "fired" on a continual and consistent basis will help us to keep our course correct and prevent our lives from spinning out of spiritual control.

SEVEN QUESTIONS THAT YIELD GOLD

Back to the mining analogy: Picture yourself in a mine, looking at a rich vein of silver or gold. Now, if you do nothing, that gold will stay embedded in that rock forever. But if you take a pick and begin to strike at that rock, the golden nuggets soon will be flying everywhere.

I want to give you the "pick" of seven questions (that you can pass along to your children) to take to the Scriptures every time you read them. When you use these questions, what you thought was hard rock will begin to yield the gold and silver of wisdom in abundant measure. As you read a passage, use these questions to excavate the nuggets of wisdom embedded in the rock of God's Word.

1. Is there a warning to heed?

2. Is there a promise to claim?

3. Is there a sin to forsake?

4. Is there a command to obey?

5. Is there a lesson to learn?

6. Is there a principle to apply?

7. Is there an example to follow?

As you ask yourselves those questions, keep a journal and write down the answers you mine—and what God gives you, pass along to your children. Sometimes you can do it at the breakfast table or the dinner table; at other times, as you are traveling down the road; at still other times, when your children approach you with a problem. It will amaze you how many times you can reach into your pocket and begin to pull out a golden nugget of wisdom here and there to hand your children to help them solve the problems of everyday life.

Incidentally, your kids can also be trained to have their own quiet time using these same techniques. At least a portion of the hour that my sons have to get ready for the breakfast table is to be spent in reading the Bible and prayer. They have even taken up my habit of reading Proverbs daily!

DON'T JUST GIVE IT, LIVE IT

One final word about passing wisdom down to your children. Your children must not only hear wisdom taught; they must *see wisdom lived.* That is why your time with God every day is so important. It is that time spent alone with the Lord that not only gives you wisdom, but also strengthens your heart. The devotional life consistently practiced is critically important.

Four ministers were discussing the pros and cons of various Bible translations. Each one gave his opinion on which version was best. The first minister said he loved the *King James Version* because of its beautiful Old English style. The second minister said he preferred the *New American Standard Bible* because of its linguistic accuracy in relation to the original Greek and Hebrew. The third minister said his favorite was the paraphrased *Living Bible* because of its easy-to-understand wording. The fourth minister said, "The best translation of the Bible I have ever come across is my dad's. He put the Word of God into practice every day, and it is still the most convincing translation I've ever seen."

Dad, when your children can say that about you, that is when you will know you have really struck gold!

DO YOU KNOW THE AUTHOR OF THE BOOK?

May I get personal with you for a moment? I want to say to any dad reading this chapter who may never have committed his life to Christ: If you do nothing else the rest of your life, would you put this

186

book down and commit your life to Jesus Christ right now? You see, you cannot live the Bible until you know the One who wrote it, and you come to know Him only through His Son, the Lord Jesus Christ.

Did you know that when a father is an active believer in Christ, there is about a 75 percent likelihood that his children will also become active believers? But if only the mother is a believer, this likelihood is dramatically reduced to 15 percent.[7]

Think about it, dad: *If the Bible is true and heaven is real and Jesus Christ is who He said He was, then for you to fail to make it to heaven—or to fail to make sure your children do—is the greatest failure possible as a father.* If you have never trusted Christ, I would invite you right now to pray this prayer:

> Lord Jesus, I confess I am a sinner. I repent of my sin
> and turn away from it. I surrender my life to you and
> receive you as my Lord.[8]

Dad, your children deserve a Christian father who will model the Christian life before them, teach them the truth of God's Word, and show them how to receive the free gift of eternal life. It could be that, in your family, this beautiful tradition will begin with you when you commit your life to Jesus Christ.

THE GREATEST GIFT OF ALL

As I have pondered why I have written this book and why I hope many dads will read it, the answer came to me in an editorial that appeared in *Texas Business*. The editorial concerned baby boomers, but I think it applies to all of the younger generation.

> We are truly the lost generation, huffing and
> puffing down the fast track to nowhere, always look-
> ing to the $ for direction. That's the only standard
> we recognize. We have no built-in beliefs, no ethical
> boundaries. Cheat on your taxes, just don't get

187

caught. Cheat on your wife, just don't get AIDS, simply use a condom.

"Where did I go wrong?" is the traditional wail of parents of kids gone wrong. The eighties version says, "We gave him everything—clothes, a computer, a car, a college education." Everything but a conscience. We are products of a high-tech society: amoral automatons, outfitted with calculating brains and slick casings, just like the computers with which we are so compatible.

But they forgot to give us souls.[9]

Dad, at the risk of beating the drum one time too many, the greatest thing you will ever give your children is wisdom from God, for the reward of wisdom is this: "Then you will understand the fear of the LORD, and find the knowledge of God (Prov. 2:5).

You cannot give your children two greater rewards than the fear of the Lord and the knowledge of God. They must fear the Lord before they can know Him, but they must also know Him before they are prepared to live for Him in the present and meet Him in the future.

R. A. Torrey was a great Bible teacher who lived at the turn of the century. He made a statement that should shake all of us dads to our very toes: "A man's success as a Christian leader cannot be determined until one sees his grandchildren." Dad, *you are not only raising sons and daughters, you are raising future fathers and mothers.*

I want to share with you first a story, and then a prayer. Gordon MacDonald told the story:

Among the legends is the tale of a medieval sidewalk superintendent who asked three stone masons on a construction project what they were doing. The first replied that he was laying bricks. The second described his work as that of building a wall. But it was the third laborer who demonstrated genuine esteem for his work when he said, "I am raising a great cathedral."

188

Pose that same question to any two fathers concerning their role in the family, and you are liable to get the same kind of contrast. The first may say, "I am supporting a family." But the second may see things differently and say, "I am raising children." The former looks at his job as putting bread on the table. But the latter sees things in God's perspective: He is participating in the shaping of lives.[10]

Fellow dads, that is exactly what we're doing—shaping lives today that tomorrow will be shaping the lives of future generations. Let's do our best by giving them God's best.

The following prayer was one General Douglas MacArthur offered on behalf of his son. I pass it along to you as my prayer for my children and for yours:

> Build me a son, O Lord, who will be strong enough to know when he is weak and brave enough to face himself when he is afraid; one who will be proud and unbending in honest defeat, and humble and gentle in victory.
>
> Build me a son whose wishes will not take the place of deeds; a son who will know Thee—and that to know himself is the foundation stone of knowledge.
>
> Lead him, I pray, not in the path of ease and comfort, but under the stress and spur of difficulties and challenge. Here, let him learn to stand up in the storm; here, let him learn compassion for those who fail.
>
> Build me a son whose heart will be clear, whose goal will be high; a son who will master himself before he seeks to master other men; one who will reach into the future, yet never forget the past.
>
> And after all these things are his, add, I pray, enough of a sense of humor so that he may always

be serious, yet never take himself too seriously. Give him humility, so that he may always remember the simplicity of true greatness, the open mind of true wisdom, and the meekness of true strength.

That I, his father, will dare to whisper, "I have not lived in vain."[11]

Dad, that is my prayer for my sons—and for your sons and daughters as well. May God above give us the wisdom to go to the True Source of wisdom, and to pass that wisdom along to the next generation.

Epilogue

THE DAD'S HALL OF FAME

Could I climb the highest place in Athens,
I would lift my voice and proclaim:
"Fellow citizens, why do you turn and scrape
every stone to gather wealth,
and take so little care of your children,
to whom one day you must relinquish it all?"
—Socrates

Proverbs is actually the first of a trilogy of biblical books written by Solomon; the last (chronologically) is Ecclesiastes. Most likely, this work was written when the king was in the later stages of his life.[1] Like Proverbs, it, too, is a distillation of divine wisdom as it has been tested in the crucible of life.

I have read it at least two to three times a year for as long as I can remember, but I guess my sensitivity to Solomon's writing as a father in Proverbs caused me to see something recently that I had never before seen in all my years of reading. It was a discovery that both amazed and excited me.

Solomon's last book could almost be characterized as one long, negative commentary on the vanity of life in general. Whether it comes to the intellectual pursuit of knowledge, the physical pursuit of pleasure, or the material pursuit of wealth, Solomon could say, "Been there, done that, and it's the same ol' same ol'."

So this grizzled old veteran of living came down to writing his last recorded words in chapter 12. I was reading his book, coasting along on cruise control, when *it happened.* All of a sudden my eyes widened, and the zoom lens of my vision focused on two words in verse 12: "And further, *my son.*" Do you see it? At the end of his life and literary career, he was still writing and talking to his son! He may have been old enough to be a grandfather, but he was still young enough to think like a father.

LIFE'S TWO GREATEST LESSONS

Years earlier Solomon had written to his son on every vital subject, ranging from sex and money to alcohol and work. Now, penning his last divinely inspired thoughts, he wrapped up his life's message with the words every congregation loves to hear the preacher say during his Sunday morning message: "Let us hear the conclusion of the whole matter" (12:13).

What is the "conclusion"? It is the life message every Hall of Fame dad must pass on to his children: "Fear God and keep his commandments, for this is man's all" (vv. 12b–13). In other words, Solomon was saying, "Son, when it comes to God, *trust and obey.*"

Dad, whatever else you teach your kids, give to your kids, or do for your kids—if you want to be in the Dad's Hall of Fame—you *must* lead them to love, trust, and obey God . . . or else your fatherhood, *from an eternal perspective at least,* has been in vain. Please, if you don't remember anything else I have said in this book, remember this!

It is no coincidence that Solomon ended his last book where he began his first one (Prov. 1:7), by admonishing his son to fear the Lord. Love for God begins with the reverence that is due Him. In turn, the person who learns to fear the Lord will pay attention to His Word and obey it. That, in sum, is the life of wisdom: fearing God and doing His will.

A DESTINY DETERMINING DAD

Dad, there is an overarching reason why I wrote this book with all of the passion of my heart. It is the sobering and staggering truth of Solomon's last written words: "For God will bring every work into judgment, including every secret thing, whether good or evil" (Eccles. 12:14).

Fatherhood is more than conceiving a child, feeding, clothing, and educating him, and sending him out on his own. Dad, *we have the responsibility of preparing that child for his eternal destiny of meeting God.* We are to make sure our earthly sons are prepared to meet their Heavenly Creator, assured of spending eternity with Him.

So I want to leave you with some suggestions—no, make that exhortations—that I believe will put you into the Dad's Hall of Fame.

1. BE A DAD WHO MODELS THE FEAR OF GOD IN HIS OWN LIFE

A cartoon punchline read, "No matter what you teach the child, he insists on behaving like his parents." John Maxwell was right when he said, "We teach what we *know*, but we reproduce what we *are*."[2] Kids may sometimes doubt what you say, but they will always believe what you do! Therefore,

- If you want your kids to have a quiet time, *you* have a quiet time.

- If you want your kids to be in church, *take* them, don't *send* them.

- If you don't want your children using foul language, watch *your* mouth.

- If you don't want your kids to drink, *you* leave it alone.

2. LEAD YOUR KIDS TO GOD AS EARLY AS POSSIBLE

You may not be a pastor like me, *but you are the spiritual leader in your home*—you should take the lead in leading your children to Christ.

- Begin when they are young and read Bible stories to them each night. Let them hear you pray for them to know Jesus personally, constantly thanking Jesus for dying for their sins, and being raised from the dead.

- As you take them to church, explain what the various rituals and seasons (baptism, the Lord's Supper, Easter, Christmas) represent and why they are observed and celebrated.

- Be sensitive to every spiritual question they ask and take the time to answer their questions thoroughly and in a way they can understand.

- Buy them Christian videos and cartoons that will present Bible truths on their level.

- Trust the Holy Spirit to give you wisdom at the right time to present the gospel to them, and pray for their salvation continuously.

On one occasion Dwight L. Moody reported "two and one-half conversions" at a service he conducted. One person said, "I suppose you mean two adults and one child." "No," Mr. Moody replied. "I mean two children and one adult. The children can give their whole lives to God, but the adult has only half of his left to give." How true!

3. PRAY SPECIFICALLY FOR YOUR KIDS AND TRUST YOUR KIDS TO GOD

I pray specifically for my sons each day; some of the requests are similar (for all three I pray for wisdom, sexual purity, their future mates, and their life's vocation), while others are tailored for each child, according to his particular needs. *I am convinced you can do nothing greater for your kids (and future generations) than to pray for them continuously.*

This was driven home to me in a tremendous story I read a few years ago about George McCluskey. I had never heard of him, but I was to learn he has had a great influence on me and my family.

As McCluskey married and started a family, he decided to invest one hour a day in prayer, praying for his kids to come to Christ and later lead godly homes themselves. Soon he decided to expand his prayers to include his future grandchildren and even great-grandchildren. Every day between 11 A.M. and noon, he would pray for three future generations.

Eventually, his two daughters committed their lives to Christ and married men who entered full-time Christian ministry. The two couples gave him five grandchildren, four girls and one boy. The four girls each married ministers, and the boy became a pastor.

The first two children born to this generation were both boys. Upon graduation, these two cousins went to the same college and became roommates. One of the boys decided to enter the ministry, but the other one didn't. He knew the family history but chose not to continue the family legacy. He became the first member in four generations not to enter the ministry and was looked upon somewhat as the black sheep of the family.

This young man instead decided to pursue his interest in psychology. After earning his doctorate, he wrote a book to parents that became a best-seller. In fact, he wrote several more best-sellers, started a radio program, and is now heard all over the world on more than a thousand stations a day. His name? James Dobson, the preeminent leader of the profamily movement for the last twenty years—and the direct result of the prayers of a father who preceded him by four generations![3]

Yes, Dad, it pays to pray!

THE FATHER YOUR CHILD CAN HAVE

Well, Dad, I have enjoyed the journey; I hope you have as well. Thanks for taking the time to let me into your heart and home. It's a tough job being a dad in a world where peer pressure feels as if it's crushing down on us at a million pounds per square inch, where values are at an all-time low and immorality at an all-time high. But what a time to be a difference-making dad! There is an enormous vacuum in this nation, aching to be filled with people who will once again stand for the values and virtues that made our country great.

Some time ago, someone wrote a little piece titled "What America Needs." I thought the author put it perfectly. America needs:

- A leader like Moses who was determined to obey God no matter what.

- Army generals like Joshua who knew God and could pray and shout things to pass rather than blow them to pieces with atomic energy.

- Politicians like Joseph who walked with God and sought His will for all policies.

- Preachers like Peter who had the courage to look people in the eye and say, "Repent or perish" and denounce personal as well as national sins.

- Mothers like Hannah who would pray for their children and give them to God, rather than become delinquent mothers of delinquent children.

- Children like Samuel who would talk to God in the hours of the night and honor their parents in the hours of the day.

- Physicians like Luke who would not only care for physical needs and treat human life both in and out of the womb as something sacred, but would also introduce their patients to the Great Physician, the Lord Jesus Christ.

- A God like Israel's, not the man upstairs, but a thrice Holy God who blesses holiness and curses sinfulness.

- A Savior like Jesus who can save anyone at any time, at any place, including an entire world, if they would just turn to Him.[4]

I would add to this list that America needs strong, committed, godly dads with the integrity, convictions, and dedication to teach their kids that in a world often headed the wrong way, God's way is the right way.

Dad, divine wisdom is the only answer to human foolishness. I encourage you to use Proverbs as a starting point and take the food of God's Word and feed it to your children, from the time they are hatched to the time they leave the nest.

C. Everett Koop, the former surgeon general of the United States, has soberly observed: "Life affords no greater responsibility, no greater privilege than the raising of the next generation."[5] When our homes become factories of divine wisdom manufacturing wise children, this nation can be turned around—and the head of that factory is to be you, Dad.

So let's get our feet off the desk, loosen our ties, roll up our sleeves; and with God's Word guiding us, let's give our kids the wisdom they need to meet the challenges of life wisely. Solomon knew long ago what we should know now: Divine wisdom, practically and parentally imparted on a consistent basis, will turn your child into a champion for God. That is my prayer for my children—and for yours as well.

NOTES

INTRODUCTION

1. *The Atlanta Journal/The Atlanta Constitution*, 5 May 1992.

CHAPTER 1

1. Warren Wiersbe, *Preaching and Teaching with Imagination* (Wheaton, Ill.: Victor Books, 1994), 237.

2. Maureen Downey, "Restoring Fatherhood Can Benefit U.S. Culture," *The Atlanta Journal/Constitution*, 29 May 1995.

3. Ibid.

4. Don Feder, "Fatherless Families Fuel Crime Explosion," *Conservative Chronicle*, 21 November 1993; italics added.

5. Ibid.

6. Dick Williams, *The Atlanta Journal*, n.d. (italics added).

7. See Stephen R. Covey, *The Seven Habits of Highly Effective People* (New York: Simon and Schuster, 1989), 95–104.

8. Gary Smalley, *The Hidden Value of a Man* (Colorado Springs, Colo.: Focus on the Family Publishing), 32.

9. Quoted by Ralph Reed, *Politically Incorrect* (Dallas: Word, 1994), 86–87.

10. Cited in David Blankenhorn, *Fatherless America* (New York: Basic Books, 1995), 1. The study cited was published in 1984. However, since nonmarital childbearing has increased dramatically since 1984—according to the National Center for Health Statistics, the number of births to unmarried mothers increased by 82 percent from 1980 to 1991—this estimation of "about half" is probably too low for children currently under age seventeen. Another more recent study states that "for children born in the 1990s, the figure could reach 60 percent if the divorce rate remains high and nonmarital childbearing continues its upward trend." See Frank F. Furstenburg Jr. and Andrew J. Cherlin, *Divided Families: What Happens to Children When Parents Part* (Cambridge, Mass.: Harvard University Press, 1991), 11, and Blankenhorn, 235.

11. Reed, *Politically Incorrect*, 87.

12. Cited by David Moore, *Five Lies of the Century* (Wheaton, Ill.: Tyndale House Publishers, Inc., 1995), 89.

13. *In Other Words,* May/June 1995.

14. Charles Colson, *A Dance with Deception* (Dallas: Word, 1993), 178.

15. Williams, *The Atlanta Journal.*

16. Colson, *A Dance with Deception,* 176.

17. Blankenhorn, *Fatherless America,* 16.

18. Peter N. Stearns, "Fatherhood in Historical Perspective: The Role of Social Change," in Frederick W. Bozett and Shirley M. H. Hanson, eds., *Fatherhood and Families in Cultural Context* (New York: Springer, 1991), 50.

19. Cited by Charles Swindoll, *The Finishing Touch* (Dallas: Word Publishing, 1994), 40–41.

20. Blankenhorn, *Fatherless America,* 45.

21. Pat Williams, *Go for the Magic* (Nashville: Thomas Nelson Publishers, 1995), 126.

22. Blankenhorn, *Fatherless America,* 226.

CHAPTER 2

1. David Jeremiah, *The Wisdom of God* (Milford, Mich.: Mott Media, Inc., n.d.), 73.

2. Patrick M. Morley, *The Seven Seasons of a Man's Life* (Nashville: Thomas Nelson Publishers, 1995), 58.

3. Warren Wiersbe's thought here is important to note: "Remember that the Hebrew society was strongly masculine and that primarily the fathers trained the sons while the mothers trained the daughters. The masculine emphasis in Scripture must not be interpreted as a sexist bias, but rather as a characteristic of the Jewish culture of that day, a characteristic that should no longer persist in the light of the gospel (Gal. 3:26–29)." Warren Wiersbe, *Be Skillful* (Wheaton, Ill.: Victor Books, 1995), 170.

Bruce Waltke also adds, "Elsewhere in the Old Testament the father is held responsible for his child's social, moral, and religious training (Gen. 18:19; Exod. 12:24; Deut. 4:9–11). Waltke, "The Book of Proverbs and Ancient Wisdom Literature," in *Learning from the Sages,* edited by Roy B. Zuck (Grand Rapids, Mich.: Baker Books, 1995), 59.

Robert Alden also makes this observation: "We might ask why only sons? Why not daughters? Much as we would hope that women had a higher position in the ancient world, it is simply a fact that they did not. Most decisions were made by men: the father, brothers, or grown sons of women. Sons were tempted by prostitutes, and men borrowed, lent, earned, and spent money. The men sat at the gate to adjudicate legal matters. On the other hand, consider the magnificent tribute to the noble woman at the end of Proverbs, and throughout the book note the direct (11:16, 22) as well oblique (12:4) suggestions for women. Today there is every reason for women, as well as men, to read this book." Robert L. Alden, *Proverbs: A Commentary on an Ancient Book of Timeless Advice* (Grand Rapids, Mich.:, Baker Books, 1983), 12.

4. Prov. 1:8; 3:12; 4:1; 10:1; 15:20; 17:6, 21, 25; 19:13, 26; 20:20; 23:22, 24, 25; 28:7, 24; 29:3; 30:11, 17.

5. Hadden Robinson from the foreword to Alden, *Proverbs: A Commentary,* 7.

6. H. Wayne House and Kenneth M. Durham, *Living Wisely in a Foolish World: a Contemporary Look at the Wisdom of Proverbs* (Nashville: Thomas Nelson Publishers, 1992), 12–13.

7. Eleanor Doan, *Speakers Sourcebook* (Grand Rapids, Mich.: Zondervan Publishing House, 1960), 284.

8. David C. Needham, *Close to His Majesty* (Portland, Oreg.: Multnomah Press, 1987), 8.

9. Steve Farrar, *Standing Tall* (Portland, Oreg.: Multnomah Press, 1994), 201

10. Paul Harvey, "They Gave Us Some Bad Advice."

11. Charles R. Swindoll, *Growing Deep in the Christian Life* (Portland, Oreg.: Multnomah Press, 1986), 56.

CHAPTER 3

1. R. F. Horton, *The Expositor's Bible*, vol. 4: *The Book of Proverbs* (New York: A. C. Armstrong and Son, 1898), 163–64.

2. Robert B. Downs, *Books that Change the World* (New York: New American Library, 1956), 129.

3. Charles R. Swindoll, *Active Spirituality* (Dallas: Word Publishing, 1994), 62.

4. Michael P. Green, ed., *Illustrations for Biblical Preaching* (Grand Rapids, Mich.: Baker Book House, 1989), 378.

5. R. Laird Harris, Gleason L. Archer Jr., and Bruce K. Waltke, *Theological Wordbook of the Old Testament*, vol. 2 (Chicago: Moody Press, 1980), 848.

6. Eugene H. Peterson, "Proverbs," *The Message* (Colorado Springs, Colo.: NavPress, 1995).

7. C. T. Onions, ed., *The Oxford Dictionary of English Etymology* (New York: Oxford University Press, 1966), 360.

8. *USA Today*, 28 January 1988.

9. Ronald Dunn, *The Faith Crisis* (Wheaton, Ill.: Tyndale House Publishers, Inc., 1984), 123–24.

CHAPTER 4

1. *The Atlanta Journal/Constitution*, 1 November 1994.

2. Letter to the Editor, *The Atlanta Journal/Constitution*, 16 November 1986.

3. "Condom Roulette," *In Focus* (Washington, D.C.: Family Research Council, 1992), 2.

4. "Combating Teen Pregnancy," *In Focus* (Washington, D.C.: Family Research Council, 1992), 1.

5. Centers for Disease Control, 73.2638CDC: CPS, DSTD/HIV: Atlanta, GA 30333, 13 June 1990.

6. Stuart Briscoe, *Choices of a Lifetime* (Wheaton, Ill.: Tyndale House Publishers, Inc., 1995), 95.

7. Allen Ginsberg, Sandra L. Hanson, and David E. Myers, "Responsibility and Knowledge: Their Role in Reducing Out-of-Wedlock Childbearing" (Washington, D.C.: Department of Education).

8. Elizabeth Elliott, *Passion and Purity* (Old Tappan, N.J.: Fleming H. Revell Co., 1983), 147.

9. Eugene H. Peterson, *The Message*, "Proverbs" (Colorado Springs, Colo.: NavPress, 1995).

10. Abstinence: "The Radical Choice for Sex-Ed," *Christianity Today*, February 1993, 27.

11. Cal Thomas, *The Things That Matter Most* (New York: Harper College Publishers, Inc., 1994), 82.

12. *Christianity Today*, 27.

13. *Fundamentalist Journal*, n.d.

14. Charles Swindoll, *The Finishing Touch* (Dallas: Word Publishing, 1994), 105.

15. Michael Medved, *Hollywood vs. America* (New York: Harper Collins Publishers, Inc., 1992), 116–17.

CHAPTER 5

1. Paul Lee Tan, *Encyclopedia of Seven Thousand Seven Hundred Illustrations* (Rockville, Md.: Assurance Publishers, 1979), 130.

2. "Only in America," *Fortune*, 11 December 1995, 236.

3. Bill Webber, *Conquering the Kill-Joys* (Waco: Word Books, 1986), 30.

4. *The Atlanta Journal/Constitution*, 11 May 1989.

5. "It's True: Anger Triggers Heart Attack," *The Atlanta Journal/Constitution*, 19 March 1994.

6. *Illustrations for Biblical Preaching*, Michael P. Green, ed. (Grand Rapids, Mich.: Baker Book House, 1989), 20.

7. John Blanchard, ed., *Sifted Silver* (Durham, England: Evangelical Press, 1995), 7.

8. *Illustrations for Biblical Preaching*, 129–30.

CHAPTER 6

1. Ronald M. Sailler and David Wyrtzen, *The Practice of Wisdom: A Topical Guide to Proverbs* (Chicago: Moody Press, 1992), 11.

2. Jack Van Impe and Roger F. Campbell, *Alcohol: the Beloved Enemy* (Nashville: Thomas Nelson, 1980).

3. Zig Ziglar, *Raising Positive Kids in a Negative World* (Nashville: Oliver Nelson, 1985), 29.

4. See Richard Land, "Alcohol: Some Sobering Facts," *Light*, September/October, 1994.

5. *Bottom Line*, June 15, 1995.

6. John F. Walvoord and Roy B. Zuck, eds., *The Bible Knowledge Commentary* (Wheaton, Ill.: Victor Books, 1985), 948.

7. Ibid., 957.

8. *Light*, January/February 1995, 7.

9. H. Wayne House and Kenneth M. Durham, *Living Wisely in a Foolish World* (Nashville: Thomas Nelson Publishers, 1992), 107.

10. Ronald Schiller, "Why Americans are Drinking Less," *Reader's Digest,* n.d., 48.

11. Mike Evans, *The Return* (Nashville: Thomas Nelson Publishers, 1986), 219.

12. House and Durham, 107.

13. Tom Strode, "Alcoholism Increases Chances of Divorce," *Baptist Press,* 4 October 1991.

14. Robert L. Alden, *Proverbs* (Grand Rapids, Mich.: Baker Book House, 1983), 148.

15. R. Laird Harris, Gleason L. Archer, Jr., Bruce K. Waltke, eds., *Theological Word Book of the Old Testament,* vol. 2 (Chicago: Moody Press, 1980), 927.

16. Norman L. Geisler, "A Christian Perspective on Wine-drinking," *Bibliotheca Sacra,* January-March, 1982, 47.

17. For example, the word is used in Isaiah 16:10: "No treaders will tread out wine in their presses." This refers to the juice that is being mashed out of the grapes by the feet, therefore a nonintoxicating wine. But here in Prov. 20:1 Solomon referred to it as an intoxicating drink.

18. In all but two of its twenty-three uses in the Old Testament (Num. 28:7; Ps. 69:12) it appears in connection with *Yayin* "wine" usually following it, once preceding it (Prov. 31:6), TWOT, 927.

19. Robert H. Stein, "Wine-drinking in New Testament Times," *Christianity Today,* 20 June 1975, 9-11.

20. TWOT, vol. 1, 376.

21. Stein, "Wine-drinking in New Testament Times."

22. Geisler, "A Christian Perspective on Wine-drinking," 51.

23. Schiller, "Why Americans are Drinking Less," 49.

24. *Nashville Tennessean,* 14 August 1984.

25. Robert B. Fischer, "Muddled in Moderation," *Moody Monthly,* May 1989, 10.

26. Ibid.

27. William J. Bennett, *The Devaluing of America* (New York: Summit Books, 1992), 118.

28. Land, *Light,* September/October 1994.

29. Willie W. White, ed., *Out of My Treasure* (Joplin, Mo.: College Press, 1964), 278.

CHAPTER 7

1. Patrick Morley, *The Man in the Mirror* (Brentwood, Tenn.: Wolgemuth & Hyatt, Publishers, Inc., 1989), 130.

2. Morley, *The Man in the Mirror,* 110.

3. Norman Cousins, *Human Options* (Berkeley Press, 1983), 103.

4. Stuart Briscoe, *Choices for a Lifetime* (Wheaton, Ill.: Tyndale House Publishers, Inc. 1995), 150.

5. Eugene Peterson, *The Message: The Wisdom Books* (Colorado Springs, Colo.: NavPress, 1996), 324.

6. *The New Living Translation* (Wheaton, Ill.: Tyndale House Publishers, Inc., 1996), 669.

7. Morley, *The Man in the Mirror,* 131.

8. Robert C. Larson, *The Best of Ted Engstrom* (Here's Life Publishers, 1988), 17.

9. Larry Burkett, *Answers to Your Family's Financial Questions* (Pomona, Calif.: 1987),52.

10. Dr. James C. Dobson, *Love for a Lifetime* (Portland, Oreg.: Multnomah Press, 1987), 70–71.

11. "Who's Happy?", *Christianity Today,* 23 November 1992, 24.

12. "Religious Faith: Firm Foundation for Charity," *Christianity Today,* 19 November 1990, 63.

13. John Ronsvalle and Sylvia Ronsvalle, "Giving Trends and their Implications for the 1990s," a paper presented at the North American Conference on Christian Philanthropy, Minneapolis, Minnesota, 24–27 September 1990, 1–6.

14. *In Other Words,* May/June 1994.

15. Michael Wolff, *Where We Stand: Can America Make It in a Global Race for Wealth, Health, and Happiness* (New York: Bantam Books, 1992), 24.

16. "Rising Tide of Debt," *USA Today,* 30 October 1995.

17. John Naisbitt, *Megatrends* (New York: Warner Books, 1984), 166.

18. Wayne House and Kenneth M. Durham, *Living Wisely in a Foolish World* (Nashville: Thomas Nelson Publishers, 1992), 41–42.

19. Larry Burkett, *Answers to Your Families Financial Questions* (Pomona, Calif.: Focus on the Family Publishing, 1987), 77.

20. Bill Hybels, *Honest to God?* (Grand Rapids, Mich.: Zondervan Publishing House, 1990), 162.

21. James Patterson and Peter Kim, *The Second American Revolution* (New York: William Morrow & Co., Inc., 1994), 79.

22. Dr. James Dobson, *Straight Talk to Men and their Wives* (Waco, Tex.: Word Books, 1980), 147–48.

23. Albert M. Wells, Jr., *Inspiring Quotations* (Nashville: Thomas Nelson Publishers, 1988),129.

CHAPTER 8

1. *The Atlanta Journal,* 2 September 1996.

2. Derek Kidner, *Proverbs* (Downers Grove, Ill.: InterVarsity Press), 42.

3. Robert Hicks, *In Search of Wisdom* (Colorado Springs, Colo.: Nav Press, 1995), 50.

4. A. L. Williams, *All You Can Do Is All You Can Do, and All You Can Do Is Enough* (Nashville: Oliver Nelson, 1988), 61.

5. Charles R. Swindoll, *Active Spirituality* (Dallas: Word Publishing, 1994), 106.

6. *The Atlanta Journal,* 2 September 1996.

7. Bill Gothard, *Men's Manual,* vol. 2 (Oak Brook, Ill.: Institute in Basic Youth Conflicts, Inc., 1983), 226.

8. R. C. Sproul, *Pleasing God* (Wheaton, Ill.: Tyndale House Publishers, Inc., 1988), 179.

9. *The Atlanta Journal,* 2 September 1996.

10. Gothard, *Men's Manual,* 229.

11. Ibid.

12. Larry Burkett, "Retirement Goals," *Moody Monthly,* February 1995, 34.
13. Pat Williams, *Go for the Magic* (Nashville: Thomas Nelson Publishers, 1995), 137.

CHAPTER 9

1. Justin Kaplan, ed., *Bartlett's Familiar Quotations* (Boston: Little, Brown & Co., 1992), 230.
2. Robert C. Larson, *The Best of Ted Engstrom* (Here's Life Publishers, 1988), 253.
3. Charles R. Swindoll, *Living above the Level of Mediocrity* (Waco: Word Books, 1987), 236–37.
4. *Bits and Pieces,* 14 October 1993.
5. H. Wayne House and Kenneth M. Durham, *Living Wisely in a Foolish World* (Nashville: Thomas Nelson Publishers, 1992), 101.
6. John Blanchard, ed., *Sifted Silver* (Durham, England: Evangelical Press, 1995), 106.
7. Charles W. Colson, *Life Sentence* (Lincoln, Va.: Chosen Books, 1979), 79.
8. Charles R. Swindoll, *Active Spirituality* (Dallas: Word Publishing, 1994), 129.
9. Michael P. Green, *Illustrations for Biblical Preaching* (Grand Rapids: Mich.: Baker Book House, 1989), 228.
10. Frances Brown, S. R. Driver, and Charles A. Briggs, *Lexicon* (London: Oxford University Press, 1972), 17.
11. Kathleen A. Farmer, *Proverbs and Ecclesiastes: Who Knows What Is Good?* International Theological Commentary Series (Grand Rapids, Mich.: Eerdmans, 1991), 78.

CHAPTER 10

1. Justin Kaplan, ed., *Bartlett's Familiar Quotations* (Boston: Little, Brown & Co., 1992), 299.
2. *The Atlanta Journal,* 25 September 1995.
3. D. Bruce Lockerbie, *Who Educates Your Child?* (Garden City, N. Y.: Doubleday & Co., Inc., 1980), 92-93.
4. Chuck Swindoll, *Growing Wise in Family Life* (Portland, Oreg.: Multnomah Press, 1988), 116.
5. *The Quest for Character* (Portland, Oreg.: Multnomah Press, 1987), 105-106.
6. H. Wayne House and Kenneth M. Durham, *Living Wisely in a Foolish World* (Nashville: Thomas Nelson Publishers, 1992), 68.
7. Zig Ziglar, *Raising Positive Kids in a Negative World* (Nashville: Oliver Nelson, 1985), 216.
8. Hank Tate, "Discipline—You Can't Succeed Without It!" *In Other Words,* November/December, 1994.
9. R. Laird Harris, Gleason L. Archer Jr., and Bruce K. Waltke, eds. *Theological Wordbook of the Old Testament,* vol. ii (Chicago: Moody Press, 1980), 578.
10. Ziglar, 216.

11. House, 64.

12. Walter C. Kaiser Jr., *Hard Sayings of the Old Testament* (Downers Grove, Ill.: InterVarsity Press, 1988), 180-81.

13. Derek Kidner, *Proverbs* (Downer's Grove, Ill.: InterVarsity, 1964), 147.

14. Italics added.

15. Gleason L. Archer, *Encyclopedia of Bible Difficulties* (Grand Rapids, Mich.: Zondervan Publishing House, 1982), 252.

16. Kaiser, 181. Another author put it this way: "When they reach adulthood, having been known and uniquely trained by their parents, they will not depart from the path of obedience." Charles R. Swindoll, *Growing Wise in Family Life* (Portland, Oreg.: Multnomah Press, 1988), 94.

17. Kaiser wisely reminded us: "As with many other moral proverbs of this sort, the question often comes from many a distraught parent: 'Does this proverb have any exceptions to it, or will it always work out that if we train our children as this verse advises us, we can be sure they won't turn from the Lord.'

No, this verse is no more an ironclad guarantee than is any other proverb in this same literary category. As in many other universal and definite moral prescriptions (Proverbs) it tells us only what generally takes place without implying there are no exceptions to the rule. The statement is called a proverb, not a promise. Many godly parents have raised their children in ways that were genuinely considerate of the children's own individuality and the high calling of God, yet the children have become rebellious and wicked despite their parents' attempts to bring about different results." Kaiser, 181.

18. J. Oswald Sanders, *A Spiritual Clinic* (Chicago: Moody Press, 1958), 90.

19. *Pulpit Helps,* vol. 14, June 1989.

CHAPTER 11

1. William Kilpatrick, *Why Johnny Can't Tell Right from Wrong* (New York: Simon & Schuster, 1992), 248–49.

2. TWOT, vol. 1, 126.

3. Robert L. Alden, *Proverbs: A Commentary on an Ancient Book of Timeless Advice* (Grand Rapids, Mich.: Baker Book House, 1983), 32.

4. "Survey Shows Lack of Bible Reading," *Moody Monthly,* February 1989.

5. Personal files.

6. Bill Nelson, *Mission* (New York: Harcourt, Brace, Jovanovich, 1988), 120.

7. *The Contemporary Pulpit* 7, July–September 1995, 7.

8. To any dad who may have prayed this prayer, the Word of God is your assurance that you have been saved. God has given you His word: "Whosoever shall call upon the name of the Lord, shall be saved" (Rom. 10:13).

9. Mike Bellah, *Baby Boom Believers* (Wheaton, Ill.: Tyndale House Publishers, Inc., 1988), 130.

10. Gordon McDonald, *The Effective Father* (Wheaton, Ill.: Tyndale House Publishers, Inc., 1977), 183–84.

11. Personal files (italics added).

EPILOGUE

1. "Solomon probably wrote Proverbs (Prov. 1:1; 1 Kings 6:32) and the Song of Solomon (1:1) during the years he faithfully walked with God; and near the end of his life he wrote Ecclesiastes." Warren W. Wiersbe, *Be Satisfied* (Wheaton, Ill.: Victor Books, 1990), 13–14.

2. John C. Maxwell, *Be a People Person* (Wheaton, Ill.: Victor Books, 1989), 132.

3. Steve Farrar, *Point Man* (Portland, Oreg.: Multnomah, 1990), 154–55.

4. Anonymous, personal files.

5. *In Other Words*, Winter 1996, 3.

LaVergne, TN USA
15 September 2009
157900LV00001B/103/P